A Handbook for Museum Trustees

By Harold and Susan Skramstad

Published in cooperation with
the Museum Trustee Association

AMERICAN ASSOCIATION OF MUSEUMS

© 2003 American Association of Museums
1575 Eye St. N.W., Suite 400
Washington, DC 20005

A Handbook for Museum Trustees

On the cover: George Giusti, *"Civilization is a method of living, an attitude of equal respect for all men"—Jane Addams, Speech, Honolulu, 1933. From the series Great Ideas of Western Man.* 1984.124.107. Smithsonian American Art Museum, Gift of Container Corporation of America.

Excerpts on pages 25-27 from "The New Work of the Non-Profit Board," by Richard Chait, Thomas Holland, and Barbara Taylor, *Harvard Business Review*, September/ October 1996, reprinted by permission of *Harvard Business Review*. Copyright © 1996 by the Harvard Business School Publishing Corporation; all rights reserved.

Excerpt on pages 54-55 from *What Management Is: How It Works and Why It's Everyone's Business*, by Joan Magretta, with the collaboration of Nan Stone. Copyright © 2002 by Joan Magretta. By permission of The Free Press, a division of Simon & Schuster.

Excerpt on page 138 from *National Renewal*, by John W. Garner, September 1995, reprinted by permission of the National Civic League and Independent Sector.

Design: LevineRiederer Design

Library of Congress Cataloging-in-Publication Data

Skramstad, Harold, 1941-
  A handbook for museum trustees / by Harold and Susan Skramstad.
      p. cm.
Includes bibliographical references (p.   ) and index.
  ISBN 0-931201-83-7
  1. Museum trustees—United States—Handbooks, manuals, etc. 2. Museum trustees—Handbooks, manuals, etc. 3. Museums—United States—Handbooks, manuals, etc. 4. Museums—Management—Handbooks, manuals, etc. I. Skramstad, Susan, 1942- II. American Association of Museums. III. Title.

AM11.S58 2003
069—dc21
                                          2003000300

A Handbook for Museum Trustees

Table of Contents

Table of Contents continued

Acknowledgements

IN WRITING THIS BOOK we have depended in so many ways on Alan and Patricia Ullberg's pioneering *Museum Trusteeship*, which was published in 1981 and has served the museum field for more than two decades. We have drawn very heavily from the Ullbergs' legal perspective, especially from their essay on the historical roots of trusteeship, and from both the published writings of and our friendship with Stephen E. Weil. Steve has almost single-handedly created the genre of critical literature in the museum field and for that we should all be grateful. Our perspective also has been deeply influenced by the work of Richard Chait and his colleagues, whose perspectives on the "new work of the board" have both ratified and stretched our own instincts, experience, and perspective.

We owe a great debt of gratitude to Jane Lusaka and John Strand of the AAM publications staff, who shepherded this book and its authors through the process of writing and publication with exceptional grace and endurance. We also would be remiss if we did not thank our many client organizations and individuals, many of whom have become friends and whose issues and concerns have provided so much food for thought about this field we are all in.

Harold and Susan Skramstad

Preface

IT IS AN HONOR AND A PRIVILEGE to serve on the board of a museum. And done well, it is challenging and rewarding work.

This country is blessed by a network of museums that in their diversity, size, scope of collecting, and service to the public are unparalleled anywhere else in the world. In the United States, the private sector is primarily responsible for leading, overseeing, and supporting this vast and complex web of institutions. In virtually every community, private citizens in the guise of trustees worry about the well being of the museums in their care. With enormous good will, they work hard to ensure that the public's best interests and the museum's needs are protected and addressed, now and in the future.

It is a remarkable system that places so much responsibility on the shoulders of volunteers. It is equally remarkable that the system works as well as it does. It depends for its success on the good will and good intentions of those who agree to serve on boards, on a culture of volunteerism that ingrains a sense of obligation and accountability, and on a tradition of "look and learn" that enables successive generations of trustees to make incremental improvements in the practice of good governance.

Critical as these elements are to the routine ability of most boards to do a good job, much has been left to chance. Knowledge and wisdom that should be widely available often are acquired in sometimes painful, inefficient, and repetitive ways. The work of museum trustees and the effectiveness of museum boards are too important merely to hope for the best and be grateful that the worst doesn't make the headlines.

The Museum Trustee Association serves the needs of the museum community's many able trustees by providing a forum where trusteeship, governance, and the leadership of museums can enjoy the attention they need and deserve. Our mission is unusually challenging. Unlike a museum staff or the museum itself, trustees are hard to locate. When they leave the boardroom, they assume their identities in their communities; they are members of households, parents of children, lawyers, doctors, business leaders, almost always volunteers elsewhere. There is no great computer in the sky with a button marked "museum trustee" that can print out a list of the tens of thousands of citizens who serve on museum boards.

The key to grooming stronger and more effective trustees—to helping trustees incorporate new ideas or critical information into their work—is to create a stream of information and multiple points of access that allow museum trustees and executive directors to learn and reflect on the characteristics and process of good governance. With *A Handbook for Museum Trustees*, Susan and Harold Skramstad provide an important tributary that contributes to that stream, bringing an abundance of good, clear information and advice about governance in today's museums that every trustee can benefit from reading. Their book takes trustees through the essentials of effective board practice but always in a manner that acknowledges the current complexity of effective trusteeship.

Museum governance is not easy. Although we must adhere to a set of fundamental principles and practices, the enormous diversity that characterizes the field makes generalization difficult. Every description, every attempt to provide guidance must be qualified. From board room to board room, the rules of engagement, the history, the critical issues will differ. The environment in which museums do their work is challenging and, depending on the state of the economy, sometimes perilous. Museums have taken on new roles in their communities and conduct their business in a more critical and skeptical public arena. Leadership in the field is changing. Executive directors are less likely to spend their careers in a single institution; trustees are more likely to be adept with technology and to value the speed and efficiency it brings. Big, intractable issues need our attention and the old forms of board work may not give us the best ways to address them.

As a long time trustee of the Detroit Institute of Arts and the chairman of the Museum Trustee Association, I welcome and value the Skramstads' book and applaud their long careers of service to the museum profession. This is a book that every museum trustee should read; it should be taken apart and used, as it is designed, to build conversation, encourage reflection, fine-tune performance, and create a climate in which strengthening the work of the board is the carefully tended objective of every museum.

Andrew L. Camden, chairman, Museum Trustee Association,
and trustee, Detroit Institute of Arts

Introduction

MUSEUMS ARE AND ALWAYS HAVE BEEN important institutions in American life. Our earliest museums helped define and shape the intellectual life of the nation. Today, museums are involved in a wide variety of roles that deepen and broaden our understanding of the past, the natural and physical world, and our artistic and scientific creativity.

Because museums are so important to society, their trusteeship is also vitally important. Trustees are at the center of the museum enterprise. They are the formally constituted group that legally represents the public good in all aspects of a museum's work. For this reason trusteeship is like marriage, "not to be entered into unadvisedly or lightly, but . . . in accordance with the purposes for which it was instituted. . . ."

This publication has been designed to help museum trustees better understand both the "why" and, more important, the "how" of trusteeship. It is our underlying assumption that every museum has a distinctive mission and special role in its community and that there will be great variation in the way a particular board of trustees may handle its challenges and issues. Part of our goal is to help you, as boards of trustees, and the directors of your museums understand what your critical and non-negotiable duties are and which areas of responsibility are subject to a greater variety of approach in discussion and decision. We also will provide you with some practical guidelines for improving board processes and the work of your board.

We have purposefully taken a hard line on board performance for several reasons: 1) This is a personal conversation between us and board trustees who are seeking to improve their performance, and 2) the work of the board is too important to permit anything less than clarity on the issues. We are going to show you where the "sore spots" are, probe them, and give you some suggestions for alleviating those that sound familiar to you. Our experience is very close to yours—we have both been on boards, we have both chaired boards, and one of us is a board chair right now. We are all in this together, along with museum CEOs and staffs, and we are engaged in important work that we must do well.

We take as a starting point that old rules of board governance, such as *the board sets policy; the staff carries it out*, are no longer appropriate or helpful. It seems clear that museum boards of trustees, in conjunction with the institution's senior staff, must find new ways of working together to improve museum performance, which, of course, is the goal. Museums are an extremely diverse group of organizations, and there is no best way for a board of trustees to carry out its work. Each museum has to find its own way in the world, consistent with its particular mission, strategic direction, and resources, both human and financial.

It would be an understatement to say that there are resources that can assist anyone with an interest in trustee performance, or help boards fulfill their responsibilities and work more effectively; in fact, we are drowning in opportunities for illumination. There are a vast number of publications, consultants, experts, and particular points of view available to anyone with access to a bookstore, library, or the Internet. But despite the experts, the consultants, the pundits, and the publications, the issue of effective board governance continues to be a problem in far too many museums and remains at the top of the worry list.

We believe that boards may be sinking themselves by an inattention to the basic and obvious things—the chores no board wants to bother with—every bit as often as they are sunk by big strategic issues. We have detailed both in this book in the hopes that it will help you become what we know each board would like to become: the Ideal Board for the Great Museum.

For the last six years we have focused our work as consultants on institutional change, strategic planning, and resource development and have consequently worked with a large number of very diverse boards representing a very diverse set of institutions. The conclusions we have drawn from this work inform this book from beginning to end. This book is for boards; it will be read by others but it is *for* boards. We have written it for you.

We say that, repeat it, and draw attention to it, because it has been our observation that books like this one are most often read by museum CEOs looking for ways to inspire or drive their boards to better performance, rather than by board members. CEOs are avid, even frantic, readers of how-to books on building effective boards, hoping, we must assume, that the information they consume will eventually reach its intended targets through the carefully placed suggestion. Unlikely. More directly, they also spend countless dollars providing their boards with books and pamphlets delicately aimed at "helping" them to do their jobs better, with just about as much impact. Such efforts, despite the CEO's well-meaning intentions, are pointless. The development of an effective board of trustees is a board responsibility. If the board is not willing to change, change will not occur; if it is willing, the process to change can be surprisingly smooth.

What we have observed in our work, however, is not that boards are unwilling to change but that they are unaware that they should change, need to change, or even, in some cases, have to change. If improvement is suggested, they often unite in puzzlement, irritation, defensiveness, or by ignoring the issue. A united board is a mighty force; indeed CEOs are devouring relatively dull books to find out how to unleash that very force. But, alas, what brings the genie out of the bottle to perform its powerful magic is often a well-intentioned suggestion that there is room for improvement: "The board's bylaws are out of date." "The board does not discipline its own members." "The board does not come prepared to meetings." "The board is not fulfilling its fund-raising obligations."

Boards often react to criticism defensively, and when a board unites around a defensive posture, the game is all but lost. Consequently, it is difficult for the museum's CEO to productively critique the board's performance, and many are reluctant to even try. This is further complicated by the fact that board members seldom criticize themselves or their fellow trustees. Peer relationships provide a certain comfort that's hard to give up, even though it may come with certain unproductive but accepted social norms that frown on challenge, strong disagreement, or difficult conversations. In other words, Emily Post wouldn't approve.

Well, Emily Post isn't in the boardroom, and the board isn't a social gathering. The board is made up of people charged with the legal responsibility for ensuring the successful operation of their museum. Perhaps because museum board members, unlike their colleagues in the for-profit sector, are not paid for their service, they don't take it as seriously as they might. But whatever the cause, museum board members often seem to leave their business sense at the door. Anyone with a business to protect puts civility some considerable distance after responsibility to the good of the business. If your mother's on the wrong track about your livelihood, she's on the wrong track, and you'll say so. There is no point in ruining the business to avoid a confrontation. But, more often than not, museum trustees are willing to shave both ends of an argument so that the discussion can proceed civilly. Who wants to offend a friend, neighbor, business colleague, influential member of the community, or, occasionally, a relative? Time and again we have found that a lack of comfort about open disagreement or straightforward discussion of difficult issues is often behind a problem that has festered for some time.

The museum is a business, too, and has no more room for fuzziness than does a for-profit business. Remember, not-for-profit doesn't mean that the museum can bring in less money than it spends or fail to measure its progress against its mission and goals on an ongoing basis. It simply means that its "bottom line" is the public good, not individual financial gain. The museum must be well run, attentive to its "customers," and financially sound; its performance should be monitored by the board, the media, other museums and museum professional associations, its visitors, and the community in which it is located.

Boards of trustees, however, seldom give themselves over to scrutiny from either outside or inside. While willing to examine the work of the staff, especially the CEO, with a microscope, many boards consider their own work either too important, or not important enough, to deserve serious examination, preferring the role of doctor to the role of patient. The most basic questions often remain unasked, including: Do we have the right people on this board? Is it the right size? Are there one or more members who dominate and/or intimidate the other members? Is the relationship with the CEO a true partnership? Is the museum headed in the right direction? Do we understand the needs of our audiences? Do we have sufficient resources, financial and human, to do the job? Do we really understand what our job is? Is the CEO's performance satisfactory? Is our standing in the community all that it should be?

Boards of trustees are at the heart of the success, and the failure, of the organizations they serve. Our experience has shown that although the museums of this country are distinct and different, each in its own wonderful way, their problems are very similar and often are connected to personal relationships with the museum's founder, the chair, other board members, the museum's CEO. That is not to say that there are not some major strategic issues that keep museum CEOs and their boards up at night, but relationships, the ability to speak openly and professionally about concerns, may be at the heart even of these.

Our purpose is to identify the issues that keep many boards from achieving their full potential, make boards aware of these issues, and provide ways for boards to solve their problems before they threaten their museums in a serious way.

We do not mean to suggest that the museum boards of the United States are in disarray or that they are ineffective. Many museum boards are models of what good boards should be. But many are not. The problem is that those who need help may be the last to see it. It may, in fact, be the CEO alone who is frustrated; hence the directorial nightstand stacked with books on board development. And our message to you (CEOs and board members alike) is simple—the CEO alone can do little to improve the performance of the board. But board members take note: the fact that so many CEOs are reading so many books on building better boards must mean something; they can't be doing it for fun.

We selected the handbook format because we believe that while it is extremely important to understand the issues theoretically, it is also important to have practical assistance close at hand, particularly for organizational issues. Thus we have included practical process suggestions in every chapter except the first, which provides an historical perspective on museums, American museums in particular, and trusteeship. Chapters 4 and 5 are step-by-step "how-to" chapters about forming and keeping a good board, and they are almost totally process oriented.

We have included some quick assessment tools that we have found useful in our work. These are very simple forms for such things as evaluating a CEO, criteria for selecting board members, and post-meeting surveys. They are meant to serve as a stimulus for you to develop your own assessment tools around the particular needs of your own organizations. The Museum Trustee Association has been championing and refining the assessment process for boards, individual board members, and the director for years. Its publication, *The Leadership Partnership*, cited in the bibliography, can serve as a very useful tool for boards, providing templates and a wide array of assessment formats for your use.

In the chapter discussions and practical examples we have chosen to name our fictional museum, the Great Museum, and its board, the Ideal Board. This is, after all, what boards and staffs are striving for. We refer consistently to "board members" and "trustees," but in fact these terms represent a much wider variety of legally constituted groups that may have governing authority over a museum, such as a city manager, city council, and appointed public authority. In addition, we often use the term "CEO" to indicate the paid staff person who provides executive leadership to the museum, whether that person is known as the president, director, executive director, or something else.

We believe that it is important for boards to practice the art and technique of informed professional discussion before they find themselves in a difficult situation and have to do it "for real." To that end we have included a set of hypothetical cases at the end of this book, and we encourage you to use them. Each case gives trustees an opportunity to discuss an important issue, which, hopefully, will *not* be a current problem for their board. The process can be stimulating, provocative, and fun and there is more than one answer to every question. If and when a real crisis does arrive, the board will be ready to discuss it comfortably.

We also have included a list of suggested readings in a number of areas as well as a few of the more relevant Web sites, in case you haven't had enough by the time you finish reading this.

We have heard again and again from colleagues in the museum field that the primary readers of this book will be museum CEOs. If this happens, we will have failed. As we have said before, the impetus for the improved performance of a board of trustees must come from the board itself or it won't have the will to carry it out. This book is an attempt to provide individual trustees and their boards with a better understanding of their special role and how they can fulfill that role to become the Great Museum's Ideal Board. In the end what is most important to remember is that both the museum's trustees and its staff are tools for some larger purpose—the improved performance of the institution. Issues, concerns, and conflicts should neither be about nor influenced by the special interest or agenda of either board or staff. The focus must always be on the performance of the museum. Everything else is peripheral.

We celebrate the work of boards. Without the selfless individuals that serve on them, the nation's museums would be infinitely poorer. Our intent is simply to bring to trustees' attention the key issues we have drawn from our extensive work on and with boards, and we urge each one of you to look at the boards on which you serve with the clear vision of an outsider. If you start to argue with yourself, the outsider has come up against the insider, and the discussion should be interesting.

Because of its special purpose, the museum has been granted the privilege of tax exemption with the expectation that its staff and volunteer board will ensure fulfillment of its mission in an effective and efficient way. That, in its broadest sense, is what board work is all about.

CHAPTER 1

Museums and Trusteeship: A Historical Perspective

THE PRECEDENTS FOR CONTEMPORARY TRUSTEESHIP have evolved over a long period of time, from the earliest moment that men and women realized that they were in some way responsible for one another. In ancient Judaic law, charity was recognized as an important religious and civic duty. During the second millennium B.C., King Hammurabi's code of law spoke of the concept of a trust as a way one individual could hold property for the benefit of another. Roman law made a specific provision for setting aside money or property for charitable purposes.

In Western society, both the moral and legal concepts of the charitable trust were strengthened by the Christian church; money could be given to the church for the public welfare and its administration was governed by ecclesiastical law. Over time the administration of such funds became the responsibility of secular courts. In 1601 the English Parliament passed the Statute of Charitable Uses, establishing an oversight process for ensuring the proper management of property or funds exempt from taxation because of their charitable purpose. Enforcement of the laws of charitable trusts became firmly established as the function of the courts, a concept that continues in the present day.

Formed in a nation characterized by historian Daniel J. Boorstin as creating and recreating new, transient, "upstart" communities, most early American museums were voluntary associations that brought together civic boosters in an eclectic mix of collecting, education and entertainment. Museums, like colleges and universities and theaters and opera houses, often were built and in business before roads were named or paved. They functioned to anchor the new communities for which they were created, giving those places an almost instant sense of tradition, history, art, and culture. Characteristic of these museum enterprises was a very practical bias toward community values and a governance structure that reflected a blurring of the founders' private interests and the institution's public purpose. These museums usually were governed by boards of trustees made up primarily of leading businessmen and other civic leaders, who saw the museum as essential to the development of the kind of communities that would attract others to come and to settle.

The distinguishing feature of American museums has always been their diversity. From the beginnings of the republic, American museums developed a variety of forms and functions to meet the needs of a rapidly expanding population. The country's first permanent museum was established in Charleston, S.C., created by the Charleston Library Society's decision in 1773 to "collect materials for a full and accurate natural history of South Carolina." Charles Willson Peale's "A Repository of Natural Curiosities" was formed in Philadelphia in 1786 as a private museum and soon became a major attraction in the city. By the middle of the 19th century there were a plethora of public and private museums, which, along with colleges and public libraries, were the American institutions most concerned with public education and entertainment.

If we look at the history of American museums in the late 19th and early 20th centuries, we find bold and diverse patterns of museum development carried out against the backdrop of a rapidly growing society hungry for information and knowledge. As cities such as New York, Chicago, Philadelphia, Cleveland, and Detroit became dominant centers of commerce, one of their key strategies for enlarging and displaying their economic and cultural power was the creation of large art and natural history museums. Most were founded with governance and operating structures that made them less dependent on admissions revenue from the visiting public than earlier museums had been. They relied instead on private subsidies by wealthy patrons for much of their financial support. Their founding missions combined the inspirational and the practical: to uplift and educate the public and improve the taste and skills of those who worked with their hands. The patrons of such museums recognized that museums, like libraries, universities, and symphony orchestras, were prudent investments in civic and cultural pride, an essential ingredient in the growth and success of America's emerging industrial cities.

Building these museums fell to America's new business and civic leaders. Their rapidly growing wealth, created by the vast expansion of the American economy, meant they were able to accumulate masterpieces of the artistic and cultural patrimony of Europe and the Orient, and these treasures began to find a permanent home in America's art museums. At the same time, natural history museums continued their wholesale collection of the natural world and the recording of changing and disappearing cultures. The grand museums of the great American cities—such as the American Museum of Natural History and the Metropolitan Museum of Art in New York, and the Art Institute and the Field Museum in Chicago—set the dominant tone of this movement. The size and scale of their collections was symbolic of the country's need to prove that American museums could and would reach a size and standard equal to any in the world.

The same process of museum creation was carried out in an endless number of small cities, towns, and rural areas throughout America. As the country grew and changed, local museums and historical organizations saw their role as documenting the changes by collecting artifacts and records of the pioneering past and introducing the art world and the greater scientific and natural world to the community. As American communities continued to grow and develop greater civic ambition, museums remained a major symbol of that ambition.

By the early 20th century, when public schools began to take on the role of primary provider of formal education, the educational role of museums began to receive less attention. Many museums began to consider the expansion of knowledge through collecting to be the primary focus of their work. It was assumed that the more knowledge that was accumulated through museum collections, the more valuable and useful that knowledge would be. For many museums, it was no longer necessary to be a force for popular education; rather they would be a preserver and protector of the rare, the unique, the beautiful, and the important objects of the arts, humanities, and science.

As museums continued to proliferate in the 20th century, they represented an extraordinarily rich reflection of the diversity and pluralism of American life in general. History museums, both large and small, science museums, art museums, industrial museums, and ethnic museums were all powerful tools designed to draw attention to and legitimize an extremely wide variety of groups, ideas, and achievements.

One of the most dramatic changes in American museums during the second half of the 20th century was the move toward professionalization of the museum field. That led to the formalization of the policies and procedures necessary to ensure the adequate preservation, care, and documentation of museum collections and a renewed focus on museums' educational role. It also created higher standards of performance in every aspect of museum work, emphasizing the need for professionally trained workers rather than the enthusiasts or antiquarians who had dominated the work of the field in the past.

Professionalization has been driven primarily by the American Association of Museums. Formed in 1906, AAM for many years saw itself as a convener of museum meetings and a facilitator of information within the museum field. More recently it has developed a wide variety of programs designed to improve the organizational performance of museums through accreditation, publications, consultation, self-study, and peer review as well as an array of professional training and development opportunities for individual museum practitioners. The result is that both public and peer expectations of museum performance are much greater than ever before.

For a number of years AAM had a Trustee Committee that focused on the impact museum issues had on the work of trustees; however it was difficult to find the right role for the committee in an association so dominated by the interests of museums and their staffs. Consequently, in 1986 a separate organization, the Museum Trustee Association, was formed to focus on the unique and distinctive issues important to museum boards. Over the years, MTA has grown and flourished and is an important force for the education and support of museum trustees.

Museums have been and continue to be organizations that have a deep impact on our society; they not only have reflected American life but have shaped it as well. In the 21st century the need for museums and the stories they tell is greater than ever before; for many Americans they are *the source* of grounding, inspiration, beauty, ingenuity, and pride. Nevertheless this is a world of rapid change, characterized by a highly mobile citizenry and too much work, too much stress, too much danger, and too little leisure time. The time devoted to contemplation and learning seems to have evaporated. What then will draw people in to our museums again?

Museums must be relevant to people's lives; they must be connected to their communities; they must provide experiences that can be shared by generations; they must make their experiences accessible to the rich diversity of cultures and styles that make up this wonderful country. And whatever they do, museums must operate at the highest levels of performance. Trustees and boards remain essential tools for ensuring that performance, which means that they, too, must operate at the highest levels of performance.

This book aims to give you the tools to ensure that your board is the best that it can possibly be.

CHAPTER 2

Trusteeship

WHAT ARE TRUSTEES?

Museums are part of a larger group of not-for-profit, tax-exempt organizations whose purposes are charitable, scientific, or educational. In recognition of the important role they play in advancing activities that are part of the public good, these nonprofits have been given special privileges, such as tax exemptions for the organizations and tax deductions for their donors. By granting tax exemptions and tax deductibility—i.e., relinquishing funds that would otherwise be available for government purposes—the federal government provides implicit and explicit support of nonprofit organizations. In return, the organizations are expected to fulfill their public service roles using the highest standards and in a way that benefits the public at large.

Society relies on trustees, who can be individuals or groups, to ensure that the public purposes of nonprofit organizations are effectively, efficiently, deliberately, and honorably carried out. Hence the title "trustee," or bearer of the public trust. Under the law, the trustee or board of trustees must advance the organization's public purpose, not the interests of any individual or small group of individuals. In other words, the trustees of a museum, like those of other tax-exempt organizations, must always put aside their own special interests, financial or otherwise, and responsibly represent the broad interests of the community the institution serves.

Service on a board of trustees carries the legal and ethical responsibility to use other people's money in the pursuit of an important social good. This is both a responsibility and a privilege and has been well understood throughout the historical evolution, structural development, and present situation of boards of trustees. If trustees do not perform their duties in a manner consistent with law and public purpose, the states' attorneys general and courts have a right to intervene and prescribe appropriate sanctions and penalties on individual trustees or entire boards for breaches of their public trust responsibilities.

WHAT IS A BOARD OF TRUSTEES?

What is a board really? It is a collection of individuals who come together for a common cause—such as the advancement and support of a museum—and who devote their time, effort, and hopefully their resources to helping the institution achieve its mission and vision. A board is an organism, not unlike the human body. The parts that make up the human body—eyes, ears, nose, arms, legs, teeth, feet—are different and distinct, each with a separate function, contributing to the health of the whole in a different way. But the parts do not, nor can they, function individually, and the "whole" that results from the coming together of these parts resembles none of them. The same is true of a museum board. Legally it is one body, not a group of individuals, that acts as one and is judged as one. The board as a whole is held accountable for what the museum and individual trustees do (or don't do), especially if something goes wrong.

To take the analogy of the human body one step further, if something is wrong with one of the parts, the whole suffers and the whole must act to restore the body to good health. The same might be said of a board. That is why it is so important for the board to take a proactive role in its responsibilities. When faced with a non-productive or disruptive board member, it is easy to say, "oh, he'll be off the board soon," or "he's crazy, don't worry about it," or "no one listens to her anyway." But such responses are an abrogation of the board's responsibility for the high quality of its own performance. The truth is, he won't be off the board soon enough; if he's crazy, for heaven's sake, do worry about it; and people may listen to her and believe her. In mid-2002, when it was revealed that some in the corporate world had breached their most basic responsibilities to shareholders, employees, and the public, people asked: "Where was the board while all of this was going on?" "Didn't they see it coming?" "How are they implicated?" In the end, the board as a whole is held responsible for whatever went wrong, even if the CEO or a renegade board member gets all the air-time. Maybe the trustees didn't actually do anything wrong, but where were they? Weren't they supposed to be watching the store?

It is no different in museums.

WHO ARE BOARD TRUSTEES?

Board trustees can be anyone, and they can come from anywhere. In the ideal world, all board trustees will have some or all of the following characteristics:

- They are busy people.
- They are influential people.
- They are intelligent people.
- They are committed people.
- They are effective people.
- They operate efficiently with little wasted motion.
- They understand the bottom line.
- They can bring significant resources to the table, either their own or someone else's.
- They are well connected in the business world.
- They are well connected in the political world.
- They are community representatives.
- They are willing to be part of a team effort in support of the greater good.

FUNDAMENTAL DUTIES OF INDIVIDUAL TRUSTEES

While it is important to understand that every board of trustees must operate as a unified whole, individual trustees must never forget that each board member is also personally accountable for his service to the museum. Each board member must share several common assumptions about his duties to ensure that the entire board approaches its work with a commonality of purpose that will be essential to its effectiveness. We suggest that each individual museum trustee must understand four fundamental duties to the museum: loyalty to its mission; care of its assets; service to the community; and responsibility for board performance.

1. LOYALTY TO THE MUSEUM'S MISSION: An individual that does not understand and fully embrace the mission of the museum cannot be an effective trustee. (If the museum does not have a mission statement, that is another issue and will be discussed later.) This is not to say that the mission should not be subject to regular and rigorous scrutiny. But once it is created and ratified by the museum's staff and board, the mission must be the gyroscope that guides each individual trustee's work and service to the institution. Other

loyalties, such as outside business dealings, other community responsibilities, or the potential for personal gain, must give way to the larger loyalty to the museum. From time to time, this will cause personal conflicts of interest for trustees (a topic that we'll discuss in detail in chapter 6). Even if a situation is completely within the law, it may not be ethical. Individual trustees must be aware of potential conflicts and strive to mitigate any negative effect their actions might have on the museum.

2. CARE OF THE MUSEUM'S ASSETS: In serving as a museum trustee, an individual assumes a legal responsibility and potential liability for all of the institution's assets, including its collections, physical plant, staff, financial assets, programs, and good name. As a fiduciary of the museum, a trustee takes on the responsibility of overseeing assets that have been created for the public good with other people's money. To carry out the duty of care, each individual trustee must take the time to ensure that:

- The museum's collections are appropriate to its mission and are well housed and recorded in a way that makes them physically and intellectually accessible. The collections must be appropriately used in programs and activities that advance the museum's mission and vision.

- The staff and staff leadership are appropriate to the museum's mission, qualified to do the work, appropriately compensated (both in salary and benefits), and have access to appropriate training and professional development opportunities.

- The physical plant is appropriate to the mission, well maintained, and safe for visitors and staff.

- All of the museum's programs and activities are consistent with its mission and are targeted and promoted to the appropriate audiences.

- The financial base of the museum's support and revenue is sufficient for advancing its mission and that its financial resources are expended in an efficient and effective way.

- The board listens to and continually "takes the pulse" of the community the museum serves and addresses any problems or perceived problems in a way that guarantees the continuation of the museum's good name.

3. SERVICE TO THE COMMUNITY: It is this role that increasingly defines a museum. Preservation of objects of art, history, and science are important and fundamental museum objectives. However, preserving objects is only part

of the job. Increasingly, the "so what?" question is asked of museums; artifacts are no longer seen as intrinsically good, in and of themselves. The charge to today's museums is to use their artifacts to educate, inspire, and improve the communities they serve. In the words of distinguished museum commentator and critic Stephen E. Weil, museums are moving "from being about something to being for somebody."

It is important that each trustee realize that he plays a critical role in providing a link between the museum and its community. This role, absolutely essential for every museum, can be played only by trustees, since they have a "dual citizenship" responsibility to the mission of the museum and the betterment of the community. Even in the most outward-looking museum, the CEO and staff cannot have dual citizenship because they have more clearly and professionally defined relationships with the institution. It is the role of the individual trustee to understand clearly the answer to two most basic questions:

- Why are we doing this?
- Who are we doing it for?

In addition, trustees must be able to comfortably articulate the special role the museum can and should play in the community. Trustees can be a valuable sounding board for the museum's staff and an important gatherer of information from the community. When required, they can be a living breathing survey form.

We recommend that boards stay in touch with the museum's community on a regular basis. Ask your friends, colleagues, relatives, business associates, doctors, lawyers, grocers, gardeners, visitors, the "man on the street," any or all of the following questions:

- Do you know what the museum is doing?
- Do you care what the museum is doing and if not, why not?
- Do you like what the museum is doing?
- What do you like best about what the museum is doing?
- What do you like least about what the museum is doing?
- What would you like to see more of?
- What would bring you back several times a year?
- If you do not use the museum, why not, and what would encourage you to do so?

If trustees ask these questions among their wide circles of friends and acquaintances, routinely and informally, and then bring the information back to the museum, the accumulated effect will be that the museum's staff and board will know what the community is thinking and they will never be surprised. Obviously, the same types of questions should be asked of the museum's visitors, but that is a staff responsibility.

4. RESPONSIBILITY FOR BOARD PERFORMANCE: We will return to this subject throughout the book in specific and, hopefully, useful ways. All that needs to be said here is that the board has a fundamental duty to ensure that it has the right members and strong leadership, that its members are working effectively in the service of the museum, and that any internal board problems are handled in a timely manner.

The four duties described above not only provide the foundation for the value system of individual trustees but also for the board as a whole. In the most fundamental way the essential capacity of a museum board reflects these four duties:

- The duty of loyalty to the museum's mission ensures that a shared sense of the museum's purpose guides and focuses the work of the trustees, the staff, and the institution itself.

- The duty of care of assets focuses the work of the board on its fiduciary responsibilities related to all the assets of the museum.

- The duty of service to the community focuses the work of the board on the distinctive value that the museum provides to the public through its collections, programs, and activities, and ensures a continuing connectivity between the museum and its audiences.

- The duty of improving board performance ensures that the museum will have a productive board of trustees in service to the museum's mission.

SUMMARY

The contemporary museum landscape is characterized by constant change. The days when museums were seen as havens of stability have gone. To use the jargon of the business world, museums, like every other organization, are constantly "in play," and they must review and adjust every aspect of their work to meet the needs of new audiences with new interests and new expectations.

At the same time, old audiences will continue to visit and need their museums. All involved in the future of museums must remember that their collections and expertise have value and authority that go beyond the needs of any particular time and circumstance. Finding the right balance between continuity and change, tradition and novelty, and the most effective way of ensuring that each museum gives value to the community its serves, remains a high duty for museum boards of trustees.

CHAPTER 3

Improving Museum Performance: The Role of the Board

FOR MUCH OF THEIR HISTORY, American museums have been seen as integral to the community, their primary value being that they were there. Museums provided a record of community history, served as a symbol of community wealth, or exemplified the community's interest in art or science. They were seen and revered as protectors and preservers of their collections, whatever they might be. The museum's staff often was made up of talented amateurs or others whose interest in the museum, combined with other financial sources, made the institution's sustainability possible. The board of trustees was usually a group of respected and influential individuals who shared rank and social prestige and saw the museum as an outlet for intellectual or artistic interests and their own philanthropy, enabling them to provide an important service to the community.

To show how much museums have changed since their days as self-consciously collections-focused organizations, we share with you the rules of visitation for a private museum outside Manchester, England, written by its patron, Sir Ashton Lever, in 1774:

> This is to inform the public that being tired out with the insolence of the common people, who I have indulged with the sight of my museum I am now come to the resolution of refusing admittance to the lower classes except they come provided with a ticket from some gentleman or lady of my acquaintance. And I hereby authorize every friend of mine to give a ticket to any orderly man to bring in eleven persons beside himself, whose behavior he must be answerable for, according to the directions he will receive before they are admitted. They will not be admitted during the time of gentlemen and ladies being in the museum. If it happens to be inconvenient when they bring their ticket, they must submit to go back and come again some other day, admittance in the morning only from eight o'clock till twelve.

Thankfully, such an attitude no longer prevails. There has been a sea change in society that has dramatically altered not only the cultural and political landscape in which museums operate but the expectations of museums themselves. *Noblesse oblige* has given way to "y'all come—please." As a result people now hold the conviction that:

- Museums have a fundamental responsibility to serve the public as well as their collections, which are now considered powerful and important tools for the work of the museum rather than its reason for being.

- The way museums serve the public can be as varied and diverse as the communities they serve, and each individual museum must find a distinctive mission and vision to guide it in the development and execution of its every activity.

- The museum carries out its activities at a high level of performance, focused on enhancing the lives of the people in the community it serves.

These new expectations have created a completely new set of challenges for museums and their boards of trustees. If the museum's role is to serve the public:

- How is it to do this, and in what ways?
- What is the museum's distinctive mission, and why should anyone care?
- What are the best ways to deploy the museum's collections, staff skills, and financial resources in support of its mission?
- How does the museum measure the success of its progress toward its mission?

In looking at the changed nature of the museum enterprise, every museum board should understand that in a legal sense it—i.e., the board—is the museum. Although it may delegate the day-to-day running of the institution to a professional staff, the board is the legal entity that is responsible and accountable for the museum's performance. If the collections are poorly documented or ineffectively used; if funds are not adequately accounted for; if the programs and activities of the museum are ineffective or unrelated to the museum's mission; if the staff and its leadership are not performing adequately—it is the board of trustees that will be held legally and ethically responsible.

As the need for new and more effective ways of increasing museum performance has become more urgent, the focus of much of the museum field has been on the professionalization of all aspects of its operations and programs. While this has greatly increased the quality of all museum activities, it also has led to a hardening of the boundaries between the work of boards of trustees and the work of staff, especially staff leadership. This is not surprising. One of the goals of professionalization is to establish more autonomy for the professionals, which often is evidenced by such statements as "the board of trustees sets policy, and the staff carries out policy," and "the director is the sole avenue of communication between the board and staff." Too often, this situation has allowed a museum CEO to blame the board for his own inadequacies, and the trustees to blame the CEO for theirs. Increasingly museum staff leaders and boards are questioning such rules on the grounds of basic common sense:

- How can a board set policy without the close collaboration of staff?
- What good are policies if there is no clearly defined mission or direction?
- If there *is* a clearly defined mission and direction, how can boards and staffs pursue it separately?
- How can the board continue to educate themselves about the museum without interacting with a variety of staff leaders?

These and other questions are symptoms of the need for basic change in the way museum boards of trustees and staff leadership think about their work. Professors Richard Chait, Thomas Holland, and Barbara Taylor discuss this idea in "The New Work of the Non-Profit Board," which was featured in the September/October 1996 issue of the *Harvard Business Review*. This thoughtful and helpful article should be read by every trustee. Recognizing that the museum of today is very different from the museum of even a generation ago, Chait, Holland, and Taylor argue persuasively that museum boards must change the way they think about and do their work. This "new work of the board" will require a different and stronger relationship between the trustees and the CEO. The 21st century has barely begun; this is a good time for trustees to take a look at themselves, the boards of which they are a part, and their museums.

We will discuss later how this new work might manifest itself in board structures and processes, but it is important to note what Taylor, Chait, and Holland's research has shown:

> Traditionally, nonprofit boards and CEOs have agreed that management defines problems and recommends solutions. A board might refine management's proposals but rarely rejects any. Why?

Few trustees know the industry or the institution well enough to do more, and those who do dread being labeled as meddlers or micromanagers. Board members sometimes are made to feel that asking a thorny question is disloyal to the administration. A vote on an issue is a vote on the CEO. But how can a reactive, uninformed board know what opportunities the organization is missing? And how much damage must the organization sustain before the board realizes something is amiss?

The experience of successful for-profit and nonprofit boards has ratified this; the boundaries that have traditionally separated the roles of the board and the staff leadership have become far less clear.

The critical message is that the board of trustees and the staff must work together on a continuing basis to define, discuss, and decide the important issues faced by the museum. To do otherwise would be to neglect the full power of the organization. If the board of trustees is put in a reactive position, only responding to initiatives put forward by senior staff, the museum has lost a valuable resource—the individual and combined wisdom of some very intelligent people as well as the potential for mutual learning and the powerful process of building trust and commitment between board and senior staff.

Taylor, Chait, and Holland suggest four useful activities that will allow the board to focus on what is most important for the organization:

> Make the CEO paint the big picture. The litmus test of the Chief Executive's leadership is not the ability to solve problems alone but the capacity to articulate key questions and guide a collaborative effort to find the answers.

> Get to know the key stakeholders. Boards and CEOs have to know what matters to the constituents they serve.

> Consult experts. . . . Unless trustees understand the basic economics, demographics, and politics of the industry, boards will be hard pressed to separate the trivial from the significant and the good news from the bad. The new work requires learning about the industry from many sources.

> Decide what needs to be measured. Corporate boards typically monitor a limited number of performance indicators. Those vital signs convey

the company's overall condition and signal potential problems. Nonprofit boards often lack comparable data, largely because the trustees and the staff have never determined what matters most.

To work in partnership, the CEO and the board of trustees must change the way they think about their respective roles in the museum. They must consider the fundamental things that tie them together as well as the museum's mission and how to fulfill it. Such a view of the "new work of the board" means that the old boundaries between the trustees and the staff become less clear, while the improved performance of the museum becomes a shared responsibility.

The formal process of coming to agreement on these important matters is usually referred to as strategic planning. At its heart, strategic planning is the formalization of a process in which an institution's key decision-makers devote time and attention to raising and resolving the important issues it faces. In the case of the museum, the key decision-makers are the board of trustees and the senior staff. Once the museum becomes comfortable with a true board/staff partnership, strategic thinking, planning, acting and monitoring actions is a continuous one and will become an ongoing process as will the process of identifying, defining, visiting, and revisiting those issues that are most important to the institution.

While the board chairperson and the CEO will organize and drive this process, all the trustees must be actively engaged, since, as we said before, the board as a whole is the entity with the legal and moral responsibility for everything the museum does.

Once the work of the board of trustees is seen as a continuing process of strategic thinking and planning, the primary focus for the board's efforts to enhance museum performance can be divided into six broad areas:
- Museum Mission and Direction
- Identifying, Developing, and Evaluating Staff Leadership
- Stewardship of the Museum's Assets
- Ensuring that the Museum Has the Necessary Financial Resources to Carry Out Its Mission
- Monitoring Museum Performance
- Connecting with the Community the Museum Serves

These areas of responsibility are tremendously important and will be examined in detail in the pages that follow.

MUSEUM MISSION AND DIRECTION

Traditionally a museum's organizational chart puts the board of trustees at the top and spreads out the staff below. That clarifies the functions of the institution and its power relationships, but ignores the museum's purpose. We suggest instead that the museum's mission statement be placed at the top of the organization chart. The mission is a distillation of the essence of the museum's work and should guide and focus all of the museum's activity; in short, it gives the museum its direction. Move too far away from the mission, and the entire enterprise begins to wobble. Management literature's contemporary focus on the importance of organizational mission is not a fad but a recognition that mission is the essential foundation for everything an organization—especially a nonprofit organization—does.

Simply put, the mission states the museum's reason for being. For many years museums tended to have very similar mission statements, usually beginning something like, "The Great Museum collects, preserves, and interprets . . ."

There is, in this kind of mission statement, a strongly implied sense that the collection, preservation, and interpretation of museum artifacts is an intrinsic social good understood by all. Such a mission statement harks back to the days when the trustees of museums were themselves mostly collectors and antiquarians or individuals who saw—and therefore assumed all others would see—the collections as the embodiment of certain values or ideas that were important to society.

In the much-changed world of today, that just will not do. As museum commentator Stephen E. Weil wrote in "A Meditation on Small and Large Museums, " *Museum Studies Journal* (Spring/Summer 1988):

> . . . somewhere along the line too many of us—and here I must include myself—have too frequently misapprehended what has been a strategy to be the truth. We have too often taken as a condition to the work of museums—the existence of carefully acquired, well-documented and well-cared for collections—and treated that necessary condition as though it were a sufficient condition. In developing justifications for the public support of museums, we have too often forgotten that their ultimate importance must lie not in their ability to acquire and care for objects—important as that may be—but in their ability to take such objects and put them to some worthwhile use.

What value does the institution give to society? *That* is the question, and it is being asked of every museum in the country.

The traditional museum mission statement does not answer the important question of "so what?" If there is nothing in the museum's work that is special, distinctive, and important to society, then why should it exist? We suggest that every museum mission statement should answer the following three simple questions:

- What does the museum do?
- What happens as a result?
- What is the "value added" to society as a result of the museum's actions?

If the museum cannot come up with a compelling answer to these three questions—with emphasis on the third—then what's the point?

Examples of museum mission statements that might be helpful in better understanding the "value added" to society include:

> The Lower East Side Tenement Museum's mission is to promote tolerance and historical perspective through the presentation and interpretation of the variety of immigrant and migrant experiences on Manhattan's Lower East Side, a gateway to America.

> The mission of the Japanese American National Museum is to make known the Japanese American experience as an integral part of our Nation's heritage in order to improve understanding and appreciation of America's ethnic and cultural diversity.

> In the spirit of inquiry and discovery embodied by Benjamin Franklin, the mission of The Franklin Institute is to inspire an understanding of and passion for science and technology learning.

> Henry Ford Museum & Greenfield Village provides unique educational experiences based on objects, stories, and lives from America's tradition of ingenuity, resourcefulness, and innovation. Our purpose is to inspire people to learn from these traditions in order to create a better future.

Each of these statements incorporates a social value and purpose that goes way beyond the holding and interpreting of collections.

It is our experience that the most successful mission statements are relatively short and simple and stay focused on the basic reason for the museum's existence. Attempts to enumerate key programs and activities should be resisted since they will dilute the essence of the mission. For most museums, a good, focused mission statement will fit comfortably on the back of a business card.

If the board believes that the museum's existing mission statement clearly articulates the institution's distinctive role in its community and the value of that role—bravo. If not, it is the board's job to ensure that developing the mission statement is given the highest priority.

We have found that the most powerful step in shaping a mission statement is to listen to a wide variety of people both inside and outside the museum— not only to those who are passionately interested in the museum, but also to those who are not. Board members must be actively involved in this process so they can hear for themselves what others see as the most fundamental and important value the museum brings to its community. The key here is to remember that to talk about mission is to talk about audience. No mission can be seen in the abstract; it has to be tied to somebody.

Every word of the mission statement carries a good deal of weight and so the choice of words is important. Boards and staff alike must remember that the mission statement is not a literary masterpiece; it does not have to be brilliant, catchy, or a work of art. But it does have to be descriptive and accurate since it will guide and focus everything the museum does. It also will provide a yardstick for measuring both present activities and future opportunities. A small task force of key board members and staff can be charged to collaborate on the drafting a mission statement or the revision of an existing one. Then the full board should discuss and approve any new or revised mission statement; there will (and should) be tough discussions about every word.

A mission statement should not last forever, but if it successfully captures the special role of the museum within the community, it will not, as a general rule, change dramatically. Instead it may slowly evolve to meet changing circumstances. However, it still should be reviewed at least annually, since a serious discussion of mission forces a serious discussion of many other important museum issues.

Sometimes, however, a museum's mission might change significantly to address a new set of circumstances. For example, the Strong Museum in

Rochester, N.Y., began its life in 1982 as a fairly traditional history and decorative arts museum with a very traditional statement of mission. In the 1990s, in response to a rigorous process of self-study that looked carefully at both the museum's resources and the needs of the community, the Strong revised its mission to focus more aggressively on serving children and families.

Identifying, Developing, and Evaluating Staff Leadership

The role of the board of trustees and the CEO of the museum is a classic example of "the chicken and the egg." Without strong and knowledgeable staff leadership, the board cannot effectively do its job; without a strong and effective board, the CEO cannot do his job either. But like the situation of the chicken and the egg, the museum must build upon what it has. If it starts with a strong CEO, he can play an active role, working with the board chair to build and strengthen the board. If it starts with a strong and effective board, the chances of hiring a good CEO are immeasurably improved. It is a delicate balancing act, with trust and a genuine desire for partnership providing the equilibrium.

A museum with a good mission statement has an advantage in this process because it has gone through a rigorous self-examination to produce the statement. As a result, the board already knows what the museum is about and what kind of person should lead it. The situation is somewhat more difficult when the museum lacks a mission statement or has one that does not really represent the organization. Many boards try to put something together quickly for the recruitment package, but it is as difficult to develop a strong sense of mission and direction for a museum without the skills of a professionally trained and experienced leader, as it would be to develop one without the input of a strong governing board. A mission statement that isn't expressed clearly, or seems to describe a different institution entirely, will be ineffective. And without a sense of organizational mission and direction, it is difficult for a board of trustees to find the right staff leadership. Nevertheless, finding strong leadership is essential.

Selecting a CEO

Before it begins to think about selecting a CEO, the board should do some soul searching about the museum's strengths and weaknesses; that will help them define the kind of a leader the institution needs at that particular juncture in its history. At a minimum, the board should ask itself the following questions:

- Does the museum have a clear sense of direction?
- Does the museum need to change, or should it keep a steady course?
- Is the museum facing any kind of threat, such as reduced attendance, reduced support, reduced revenues?
- Does the museum have a good staff, or will a new CEO face personnel problems from the start?
- Will the new CEO have to follow a strong and popular CEO?
- Does the museum have a strong board or a weak board?
- Is the board open to forming a partnership with a new CEO?
- Does the museum need a good fund raiser at the helm?
- Are things in such a mess that a messiah is needed?

Different times require different leaders, leadership styles, and temperament. The most important issue for a board seeking a new CEO is to consider the fit between each potential candidate and the fundamental direction of the museum. Will this person be able to build the museum using the foundation that has already been established? Or does the museum need to change its direction; and, if so, why and how?

There is no model CEO, just as there is no model museum. The critical issue is to find a match between CEO skills and museum needs and the right chemistry between CEO and board. Different institutions will have significantly different needs. A smaller institution, for example, may want to complement board skills with CEO skills, especially if the board is expected to supplement the skills of the paid staff. On the other hand, a larger organization may seek a director with the ability to provide vision and leadership for its talented but sometimes difficult professional staff. And others may look for a record as a successful fund raiser and an ability to work closely with the board during a major capital campaign.

Of course, all boards would like a CEO who has all of these qualities (and is charming and movie-star gorgeous, to boot), but the chances of finding this person are slim. That is why identifying the most important museum issues will help you identify the most important qualities to look for in a CEO.

Finding the right CEO is complicated by the fact that many museums, like many other nonprofits, change board leadership frequently. It is easy to say that personal issues should not be central to the search process, but inevitably they will color and sometimes shape it. Too often the search for a CEO is initiated during the tenure of one board chair and completed during the tenure of another. As a result, the CEO may find himself into a difficult situation and dealing with an unanticipated personality, a situation that could frustrate even the most tolerant of people.

It is important to recognize that a CEO search means a huge amount of real work for the board. The person the board wants is probably very happy in his current job, whether it is at another organization or in the museum itself. The point is that the search must be proactive, not reactive. If the museum places an ad and waits for resumes to come in, it will be dealing with applications from almost every out-of-work or unhappy museum administrator in the country. And the chances of finding the right person this way are slim. Large organizations often hire a search consultant to relieve the board of the relentless tasks associated with searching for the right CEO. Good search firms force the board to look hard and carefully at the museum's current needs. If hiring a search firm is not an option, then a group of board members should be given the responsibility to organize and carry out the search. Once the board has formalized the museum's needs, the search group should head for the telephones and talk to people they know, looking for a light somewhere.

Too few board search groups ask their museum's staff to recommend potential CEO candidates; that is a mistake. Staff members are much closer to the museum world than are most trustees and usually will have several excellent suggestions; in addition, they will have to work for the new CEO. While many boards include staff members during the resume review part of the search process, they seldom use staff as fully as they should when identifying potential candidates.

As the board assembles a group of candidates and narrows its potential choices, it is essential for the next board chair, the person who will be the new CEO's principal partner, to weigh in before the end of the process. Someone who is enthusiastically supported by staff and most trustees, but does not have a good rapport with the board chair, may not make the best CEO for the museum.

The final and most essential step in the selection process is the checking of references. Do not shortcut this process under any circumstances. Changes in the law designed to protect the reputation and privacy of individuals have made reference interviews extremely difficult; few people are willing to be entirely candid, although it is usually possible to tell when there is something unspoken in the air. For that reason, the search group should probe carefully each issue of importance to the museum as it relates to the candidate. Board members making reference calls will have to be sensitive to every nuance of the conversation and follow-up with questions that allow the interviewee to answer candidly with simple responses. If more boards did a better job of checking references, and not just those offered by the candidates, many bad CEO choices could be avoided.

The search for a new CEO looks something like this:

- Form a search committee that includes museum staff, donors, board members, and influential community members.
- Assess the needs of the museum.
- Write criteria for the type of person the museum needs at the helm.
- Write criteria for the education, skills, and experience needed for the job.
- Ask friends, relatives, business associates, educators, and museum professionals for recommendations, and for the names of others who might have suggestions. Make sure the calls go far beyond your own town and even state, if appropriate.
- Include staff in the recommendation and interview stage.
- Advertise the position in professional museum publications.
- Cull the resumes until you have five (more or less) candidates you want to learn more about.
- If possible visit, or learn more about, the institutions where those candidates currently work.
- Interview the candidates.
- Ensure that all candidates have an in-depth interview with the board chair.
- Check references.
- Talk to people who weren't given as references but are in a position to know the candidates.
- Offer the clear favorite the position.

If a clear favorite does not surface, abandon the search and begin again.

Do not under any circumstances hire a CEO for the museum solely because the search process is so much work (which it is), you can't bear the thought of starting over again. The hiring of a new CEO may be the most important job the trustees will undertake during their tenure. Weary boards should remember the adage: "short-term pain, long-term gain." Or rather, "short-term gain, long term-pain."

The Board/CEO Relationship

Much has been written about the relationship between the museum's CEO and board of trustees. As we have said before, to improve the performance of the museum, a true partnership must be created. If museum leadership is a responsibility shared by the CEO and the board, the CEO should be an active participant in developing criteria for new trustees, the recruitment of trustees, and all other aspects of the board that directly impact his work. Boards that partner with the CEO in this way have found that the CEO can be a powerful advocate, not just on behalf of the museum but on behalf of the board as well—and really, it is the same thing. It is not possible for a CEO to "pack" the board with his own supporters; it's just not realistic. But the CEO *does* spend a great deal of time outside the museum getting to know the most influential community leaders. Consequently, he is in an ideal position to know who might serve the museum well, put forward the names of potential candidates, and assess the qualities of candidates put forward by others.

Power sharing in a leadership setting is tough, and quite unnatural, but it must be done. If the relationship between the board and staff leadership is not good, museum performance will suffer dramatically. There is a widely held assumption among boards and staffs that tension between them is a normal state of affairs, and they often develop particular strategies for dealing with each other that are nothing short of amazing. Defensiveness on the part of the CEO and insensitivity and impatience on the part of the trustees are very common, and people hoard information like water in a fallout shelter. Such a situation can and will infect the museum far beyond the boardroom. Lines will be drawn, and flexibility, creativity, energy, risk-taking, and excitement will be suffocated in the process. The combatants posture; the museum suffers. And often the chasm begins with a splinter so small that at first it seems insignificant.

Many CEOs have developed an ability to blame their own inadequacies on the board into an art form, rather than seeing the board as a rich mine of experience, skill, and wisdom, invaluable to both professional and personal growth. Symptoms of this all too common disease include:

- CEO hoards information and does not keep the board informed
- CEO is defensive
- CEO and board chair do not plan together
- CEO develops board agenda unilaterally
- CEO gives no credit to board expertise
- CEO is a *professional*
- CEO sullenly acquiesces to the board instead of openly discussing issues of conflict.

On the other hand, many boards seem totally unaware of the havoc that their own arrogance, enthusiasms, and presumptions can cause in the life of a CEO. Symptoms of this disease include:

- board maintains an exclusive, club-like atmosphere
- board micromanages the staff
- board is dismissive of staff expertise
- board is critical of staff performance
- board knows only the CEO
- board plans programs and activities on its own
- board makes important contacts on its own
- board does not keep CEO informed

There is nothing worse than seeing an organization trying to function with the CEO and board members on full diplomatic alert. The time and energy devoted to such things rapidly drain the time, enthusiasm, and commitment of individual board members, the board as a whole, and the CEO. The same commitment of time and effort could have been, should have been, focused on the important issues facing the museum.

Trustees must understand that while they have all the power, they must be exceedingly disciplined in the exercise of that power if they hope to attract and keep a CEO with the experience, skills, drive, and imagination to create and sustain a high level of museum performance. But that is not an excuse for a board to abrogate its responsibilities. There is a fine line between the board using its skills and experience to mentor the CEO, and using its power to meddle. There is an equally fine line between effective governance and rubber-stamping approval, but the appropriate balance must be found if the board–CEO relationship is to be a successful one.

Even in the best partnership situation, there must be opportunities for the board to meet alone to discuss sensitive concerns, perhaps related to staff or to the board itself. CEOs and staff have these opportunities on a regular and frequent basis, since they are at the museum every day. Generally such board discussions are rare and take place in special executive sessions. Often these board discussions cause panic among CEOs and staff because they suggest that something really bad is going to happen. Boards should consider making executive sessions a regular part of each board meeting, perhaps at the very beginning, to ensure that any sensitive issues on the mind of individual board members can be discussed and either resolved or delegated for further exploration. Making an executive session a regular part of the board meeting minimizes the threat perceived by CEOs and staff, and gives the trustees an opportunity for open and candid discussion.

Museum boards should not flagellate themselves if they find that establishing and sustaining a productive and friendly collaborative relationship with CEO and staff is difficult. Large and sophisticated for-profit organizations have to confront the same issue, and there is very little evidence that they are better at it than are museums and other nonprofit organizations.

In the end, if the relationship between CEO and board is defined by the party that holds the power, the board of trustees will always win. But it will be a hollow victory; the board will have lost the most important strategic partner it has in advancing the cause of the museum.

The CEO-Board Chair Relationship

The key element in the relationship between the CEO and the board is, of course, the relationship between the CEO and the board chair. A high level of candor and trust between a competent CEO and a competent chair is a reliable predictor of success for the museum. A lack of candor and mutual trust is an equally reliable predictor of disaster and, regrettably, it is not uncommon.

Who starts it, and why? There is no way to predict. Every situation involves two, usually well-meaning, individuals, but with two different sets of personalities, needs, ambitions, focus, and drive. But we do not believe that circumstance sets the stage for problems between CEOs and board chairs. The acknowledged complications of running an organization as complex as a museum may exacerbate the issues when they rise to the surface, but the problems are often much simpler and somewhat easier to solve than a situational disaster. They are very human, and they have something to do with pride, prerogative, insensitivity, and ego.

We know that many board chairs get along just fine with the museum's CEO and vice versa; those individuals should skip this section. Unfortunately, quite a few of you reading this book will be having a difficult time. There has been a great deal written about techniques for improving the CEO/board chair relationship, but common sense and experience indicates that the personal and professional chemistry between the two leaders is the essential ingredient for success. This does not mean that chair and CEO have to be close personal friends; in fact, that is probably not a good idea. But it does mean that they have to establish a close professional relationship, based at its core on mutual trust and respect.

Each partner must invest a serious amount of time and energy into making the relationship work. The problem is that many museum boards change their leadership frequently, making constant relationship building a large component of the CEO's job. From the CEO's perspective, unless the board has a strong succession plan, he is liable to be held hostage to an ever-changing line-up of partners—a disaster waiting to happen. It is understandable for a board, especially one made up of people with other time- and energy-consuming demands, to be reluctant to ask people to serve in a leadership capacity for too long. But that concern must be balanced by the need for reasonable continuity to ensure that the investment made by CEO and board chair in developing a strong relationship can be leveraged over a reasonable period of time. (See also "Succession," our discussion of term limits in chapter 5.)

Although the trend in many museums and other nonprofits is to limit the terms of board members, there is little evidence that better museum performance will be the result. Yes, the shortening of trustee tenure has helped boards unwilling or unable to discipline non-performing or disruptive members. But it also has created a situation in which the burden on the CEO to create and re-create strong relationships of trust and respect with the board's chair and members has become much heavier and more time consuming.

Disagreements between the CEO and the board chair are bound to occur. That is not necessarily a bad thing. Differences of opinion often lead to creative solutions to problems that are far better than either person could have developed on his own. What is important is *how* the CEO and board chair work to resolve their differences. The tradition of rigid museum board-museum staff boundaries is counterproductive to good honest debate. It encourages CEOs to hide behind their professionalism and expertise, and board chairs to retreat into an "I am the boss" mode. Neither attitude helps solve a problem or leads to a thoughtful and full discussion of an issue. Nothing beats the tried and true method of talking through a problem, when each party is required to give a little and listen attentively to the other.

There are myriad examples of boards that do not seem able to attract, or keep, a good CEO; usually they are puzzled by the problem. The museum is a wonderful place; it should attract many capable applicants. Where are they? The answer is that the museum field is like a very small town; everyone either knows everyone else, has heard of them, read their articles in professional journals, has been visited by them, worked with them on professional committees, served with them on MAP visits or accreditation visits, or heard them speak at professional meetings. And this small world of museums has a communication network that is astonishing in its efficiency. Even museums at which the staff have not talked to each other in years will know every trip, stumble, and achievement of their colleagues in the field, usually within a nanosecond of its happening. A museum with a difficult board will be well known to the field at large and will have a hard time attracting a first-class CEO.

One of our favorite stories is about the museum that had three CEOs in a very short period of time and was in the middle of what appeared to be a failed search process for a fourth. No one wanted to take the job. The board was baffled. The museum had an excellent reputation, a wonderful collection, and a substantial endowment. The consultant the board hired also was baffled—for about five minutes. Then he began to interview the staff. He heard that the board chair maintained an office in the museum and encouraged staff to bypass whatever CEO happened to be in place; what was a board chair for, after all, if not to solve the museum's problems. The CEO was often not even privy to what was going on in the museum; staff members who risked going to the CEO soon discovered that he held virtually no power. The board chair was effectively in charge. The answer to the problem was quite simple to an outside observer. But the board of trustees admired and respected their peer, the chair; they were not about to admit, at least not publicly, that the situation was harming the museum. The consultant, the only one willing to risk his job, painted a clear picture for the board chair and the trustees. They listened politely, thanked him politely, fired him politely, and changed nothing.

There is no simple formula for developing a strong and positive partnership between the CEO and board chair. A great deal is dependent on chemistry, yes, but so much more is the result of the mutual respect that can come only from an investment of time and trust, as the two parties work together to improve the museum.

Evaluating the CEO
The evaluation of the museum's CEO is one of the least understood, and most often neglected, board responsibilities. This is ironic because a great deal of care usually goes into the selection of CEOs. But once they are hired, too often they are kicked off the pier into the water. And if it turns out they can't swim, no one tosses out a life jacket because no one has stayed on the pier to watch. If the CEO wants to keep his job, or wants to please, or lacks the insight to know that all is not well, he may not even mention that he is drowning until he hits bottom. Exhausted by the process of selection the board can, and often does, neglect to begin the performance review process immediately. If the CEO appears to be doing a passable job, why rock the boat? If the CEO appears to have a few weaknesses, why hurt his feelings? Maybe he'll improve. Denial is one of the most amazing of all human characteristics. You may decide to "hear no evil, see no evil, speak no evil," but museum performance will decline as a result.

It is astonishing how many museum CEOs are unaware that their performance is a serious issue for the board until they are fired or severely censored. For whatever reason, and taking into account the very real possibility that the CEO himself was engaging in denial, the decision usually comes with little or no warning. This situation often occurs, ironically and tragically, because the museum board is unwilling to communicate its real concerns to the CEO, the first step to helping him improve his performance.

The scenario generally goes like this: slowly but surely, the board becomes less confident in the CEO. The board keeps hoping that things will get better, and no one likes the idea of bringing up unpleasant things. But things don't get better. Since the CEO attends all board meetings, and the board has not incorporated regular executive sessions into every meeting, trustees never discuss the problem as a group. The telephone wires and lunch conversations are red hot, but no one discusses the issue with the CEO. Finally, performance and trust reach a point where the situation is beyond repair. Some crisis may precipitate the reaction: bad press, a complaint by an influential member of the community, a budget deficit, or something inappropriate sent out on the museum's letterhead. And then there it is all of a sudden, visible and sitting in the middle of the board table—the elephant no one wanted to acknowledge. And the board must take action. The heedless and lucky board can get away with a severance payment and bad feelings on both sides. The heedless and unlucky board will end up with a lawsuit, ugly publicity, and a large financial settlement—none of which will be helpful to the trustees or the museum.

This situation generally can be avoided by ensuring that a formal evaluation process for the museum's CEO is in place and conducted on an annual basis at the very least, and far more frequently during any problem period. Such an evaluation should be undertaken by the chair of the board and a selected group of trustees who, hopefully, are blessed with the skills of common sense, candor, and honesty. They do no service to the CEO or the museum if they are less than thorough in their evaluation. It is important that board and CEO agree beforehand on the criteria for evaluation, generally a year before the evaluation takes place, and that the criteria are written down so that there are no surprises down the road. It is also important that the CEO be given a chance to do a self-evaluation based on the same criteria; both evaluations comprise a part of the formal evaluation process. Such criteria usually cover general areas of focus and can be listed on a form similar to the one found on pages 42-45.

Many boards find it useful to talk to key stakeholders, community leaders, and heads of organizations with which the museum works as part of the evaluation process, and we recommend that others take this approach as well. Many good boards also interview selected staff during the process. Keep in mind that there can be more than one agenda at work when a staff person participates in the evaluation of the CEO. Yet there is no denying that the staff see a side of the CEO that is often not visible to the board or individual board members.

Our bias is toward a full evaluation of the CEO, as described above, and we encourage boards to engage in this deeper type of evaluation. There is no denying that this is more work, but these varying points of view will allow the board members doing the evaluation to assemble a complete picture of the CEO's performance.

CRITERIA FOR EVALUATING THE CEO

	1) Agree Strongly	2) Agree Somewhat	3) Disagree Somewhat	4) Disagree Strongly
Board Relations				
a) Works effectively as part of a team that includes the board chair and board members, committees, and task forces				
b) Provides appropriate, adequate, and timely information to the board				
c) Provides appropriate staff support to the work of the board committees and task forces				
Strategic Direction				
d) Ensures that the museum has an appropriate mix of programs and activities for advancing its mission and vision, consistent with the financial resources available				
e) Ensures that all museum activities are monitored and evaluated against mission and goals, with appropriate qualitative and quantitative measures				
Leadership				
f) Shows initiative in all aspects of his work				
g) Demonstrates maturity and judgment in all aspects of his work				
h) Stays up to date on information, trends, and activities that are important to the museum's work				
i) Recruits and develops a diverse staff appropriate to the museum's work				

	1) Agree Strongly	2) Agree Somewhat	3) Disagree Somewhat	4) Disagree Strongly
j) Encourages staff development and education and helps program staff connect their specialized work to the museum's overall agenda				
k) Develops and maintains an organizational culture that attracts, keeps, and motivates a diverse and highly qualified staff				
l) Serves as an effective spokesperson for the museum; represents the programs and point of view of the museum to other organizations and the general public				
m) Establishes, develops, and maintains sound working relationships and cooperative arrangements with appropriate stakeholders, community groups, and other organizations that can help advance the museum's mission and vision				
General Management & Legal Compliance				
n) Divides and assigns work effectively, delegating appropriate levels of freedom, authority, and responsibility				
o) Establishes and utilizes appropriate museum structures and processes to develop an effective and efficient staff team				
p) Ensures that a job description for each museum function is developed and that performance evaluations of staff are carried out on a regular basis				

	1) Agree Strongly	2) Agree Somewhat	3) Disagree Somewhat	4) Disagree Strongly
General Management & Legal Compliance				
q) Ensures compliance with museum personnel policies as well as local, state, and federal regulations on workplaces and employment				
r) Ensures that employees are licensed and credentialed as required and that appropriate background checks are conducted				
s) Ensures that the museum maximizes volunteer involvement in all appropriate areas				
t) Ensures adequate control and accounting of all funds, including developing and maintaining sound financial practices				
u) Works with the staff and board to develop the budget; provides oversight to ensure that the museum operates within the budget				
v) Maintains official records and documents and ensures compliance with local, state, and federal regulations and reporting requirements (such as annual information returns, payroll withholding and reporting, etc.)				
w) Ensures that funds are disbursed in accordance with legal, contract, and donor requirements				

	1) Agree Strongly	2) Agree Somewhat	3) Disagree Somewhat	4) Disagree Strongly
Fund Raising				
x) Works with the board and appropriate staff to develop and implement realistic yet ambitious fund-raising plans and goals				
y) Works effectively with the board and appropriate staff in fund-raising efforts				
z) Works with the board to establish, develop, and maintain positive relationships with appropriate individual, government, foundation, and corporate donors, and potential donors				

45

The process should not be seen by the CEO as a nail-biting experience but as an opportunity to gain insight about himself and, more important, to find ways of improving performance. In fact, while there are formal criteria for the evaluation, it should not be seen as a test but rather as a process for improving museum performance and for growing and deepening the CEO's management and leadership skills. The evaluation interview offers an opportunity for the responsible board members to talk seriously and confidentially with the CEO about his frustrations and any other really important issues. Certainly it is not a time to pry into the personal life of the CEO, but it may come up; personal and organizational issues often are intertwined and if they are in strong conflict, CEO performance will suffer.

Many CEOs find it helpful to talk to the board about their performance and role as well as the concerns they have about the museum in the setting of trust and confidence offered by an evaluation interview. Some of the questions the board might use when talking to the CEO are:

- What have been your greatest difficulties and frustrations in carrying out the responsibilities of your job during the past year?
- What have been your greatest achievements
- What do you think are your greatest strengths as CEO?
- What do you think are your most serious weaknesses?
- How do you plan to improve your weaknesses?
- What parts of your work as CEO do you find most personally rewarding?
- What parts of your work do you find least personally rewarding?
- How can the board support your work as CEO?
- What do you see as your most important personal goals for the coming year?

The toughest evaluation is always the first one. The most important thing to remember is that it must be done, it must be done regularly (at least once a year), and its outcome must be a plan, agreed to by both the CEO and the board, to address important issues. The evaluation process may lead directly into other processes, such as informal mentorship or specific kinds of education or training to help the CEO address problems and grow and develop personally and professionally.

The CEO evaluation process also can bring to light failings on the part of the board or individual board members. If the board is willing to listen, the evaluation process can be a powerful tool for improving both CEO and board performance.

STEWARDSHIP OF THE MUSEUM'S ASSETS

Museum Collections

Care for collections of objects that document the natural and manmade world remains a critical function of museums. Most museums are collecting organizations, and the care, preservation, intellectual organization, and utilization of the collections is a major responsibility and ongoing cost. In a theoretical sense the museum's responsibility is to maintain its collections in perpetuity. Since that is a very long time, it is essential that the board understand the connection between the collections and the fulfillment of the museum's mission, and ensure several key things in that regard:

• Are the existing collections and the focus of ongoing collecting plans consistent with the mission? While this sounds obvious, many, if not most, museum collections have grown and developed as a result of the personal passions of staff or patrons and the vagaries of time and circumstance. While this has resulted in many extraordinary individual acquisitions and, indeed, collections, it also has created a situation in which large numbers of collection materials are quite unrelated to the museum's mission. They continue to be housed and preserved at great expense, claiming funds that could be used for activities that more effectively and efficiently advance the mission.

• If some objects are "out of the scope" of the mission, is there a thoughtful and formal process to identify such material and remove it from the collection? For some museums, the "deaccessioning" and disposal of collection items remains a controversial issue. However, the continued stewardship of materials unrelated to the museum's mission is clearly counter to the board's duty of care to those collections that do reflect and advance the mission. Some museums that are part of larger government entities cannot by law deaccession and dispose of collection materials. However those institutions that can must do so, if they are to be good stewards of both the museum's collections and its financial resources.

• If the museum deaccessions and then disposes of materials from its collection, does it consider the needs of other museums, which may be able to use such materials to fill gaps in their own collections? Does it also recognize that the material may have substantial financial value and that to transfer it to another nonprofit may violate the fiduciary responsibility that the board has to the institution and its assets? If the museum disposes of materials by private sale or auction, are there policies and procedures to ensure that no individual, and especially no board or staff member, will benefit from the sale? Here the board should be led by the CEO, who will be familiar with the norms of museum practice. But no trustee or board should ever hesitate to ask the "stupid" question; if the practice or policy sounds contrary to common sense, it probably is and should be questioned. If the answer doesn't sound right, it probably isn't.

- Is there an adequate and consistent record of the collection that allows for reasonable identification, access, and record of clear ownership? It is the board's responsibility to ensure that the museum has a system for accessing and cataloguing the collection, though each institution will develop its own system, from the vast array of generally accepted practices.

- If the museum is a collecting organization, does it own all the materials in its care? Or is it storing and preserving property belonging to some other person or organization? For the museum to spend its limited financial resources in this way is highly questionable unless there is a clear and understandable benefit.

- If the museum lends and/or borrows collection material from individuals or organizations, are there appropriate documents that ensure that the institution and its interests are protected in case of loss, injury, or some other claim resulting from the transaction? If not, the board must insist that such documents be created; otherwise, significant museum assets will be put at risk.

- Does the museum provide storage facilities and conservation measures that are adequate for the long-term preservation of the collection? If not, the board must insist that such facilities are developed and properly maintained.

Generally documents outlining the museum's policies and procedures for the acquisition, storage, documentation, loans to and from the museum, and deaccession of collection materials are gathered together into a Collections Management Policy, the overall description of the museum's stewardship responsibilities. Without such policies and procedures, one of the museum's most important assets will be at risk.

The following are some very basic and common-sense questions about the collection that board members should feel comfortable asking:

- Do we have things in our collection that are not consistent with our mission? If so, what do we plan to do about them?
- Are the museum's collections well housed, documented, and preserved? If not, why not?
- Are the museum's collections catalogued and easily accessible? If not, why not?
- Do we have collections materials in our storage facility that do not belong to us?
- Are the collections insured? If not, why not?
- How do we know how much to insure them for?
- Does the museum use the collections in its programs? Are they used by anyone else?
- What sort of things should we be collecting to advance our mission and are we collecting them? If not, why not?

The Physical Plant

Ensuring that the museum provides an attractive, functional, and safe setting for its programs and activities is an essential function for which the board of trustees is ultimately responsible. But museum trustees should not get all their information about the institution in pre-digested or filtered form; nothing beats just walking around. If trustees walk around, they will know at least half of the answers to some of the following questions, and they should feel completely comfortable about asking the others:

- Does the museum comply with all local safety and building codes? If not, why not?
- Are museum facilities physically sound? If not, why not?
- Are museum facilities well maintained? If not, why not?
- Does the museum present a clean and attractive setting for its exhibitions, programs, and activities? If not, why not?
- Does the museum have adequate and appropriate insurance to cover liability and other risks related to the public and staff using museum facilities? If not, why not?

Like every area of museum performance, the degree of active board involvement in the physical plant will depend on such things as the size and scale of the institution and any related issues or problems. If there are issues or problems, the board needs to make sure that they are resolved or solved.

Trustee Collecting

One of the knottiest issues facing the board of a collecting museum is how to deal with trustees who are collectors themselves. The issue is most difficult in art institutions but important ethical issues exist for every kind of museum collection.

The simplest way to handle the issue would be to prohibit trustees from collecting in those areas in which the museum maintains an interest. Yet for most museums such a policy would preclude any collectors from serving as trustees—a surely self-defeating policy and one that could result in a board that is insensitive to the knowledge and passion needed to forward and animate any collection-building process. Such a policy also runs counter to the common practice among museums of adding serious collectors to the board in the hopes of getting their collections during or after their tenure as trustees.

No matter the type of the museum, the resolution of the issue of trustee collecting must be guided by a shared understanding of the requirement of loyalty to the museum's mission—and that includes its collections. If that loyalty is understood—truly understood by the board as a whole and each individual trustee—then appropriate policies and disclosure procedures can be developed to ensure that individual collecting expertise and passion are not absent from the board, but channeled to the benefit of the museum. This understanding is not reached by handing out a series of by-the-book policies and procedures, but by a process of thoughtful discussion and deliberation between the board and senior staff, and by the resulting policies and procedures that grow out of a shared understanding of each individual trustee's duty of primary loyalty to the museum's mission. As we've stated before, more than anything else, open, candid, and honest discussion will help the individual museum and its board of trustees understand and hopefully avoid the potential landmines in this important area.

ENSURING THAT THE MUSEUM HAS THE NECESSARY FINANCIAL AND HUMAN RESOURCES TO CARRY OUT ITS MISSION

Money

This is one of the most obvious and traditional roles of the board. We will talk in much greater length and detail about fund raising in chapter 7. But the main point is that—under the general heading of "caring" for the museum's assets—the board must ensure that there is enough money for the museum to do its work and that those monies are appropriately and accurately accounted for, dispersed, or invested.

Specifically, the board has the responsibility to ensure:

- that the revenue and support from all sources is sufficient to exceed expenditures, so that the museum can meet its current financial obligations and invest in opportunities that further develop its mission and vision.

- that endowment funds or funds functioning as endowment are invested with the guidance of a policy that sets out quantitative expectations of overall return and is reviewed at least annually by the board.

- the performance of investment managers or advisors is monitored on a regular basis to confirm compliance with the museum's investment policy.

- that the museum's operating budget is developed in a way that reflects its priorities; formatted in a way that is clear and understandable to the board; and monitored by the board to make sure that funds are used to advance the mission and goals of the museum in an accurate, efficient, and effective way.

- that the museum's finances are audited regularly by an outside firm to certify that its financial expenditures, systems, and controls are adequate and appropriate to its operation.

People

The board of trustees must be as sensitive to the needs of the museum's human assets as it is to the financial and collection assets. Like other nonprofit organizations, museums have come to realize that, in the end, it is the people of the organization who make it a success or failure. The collections—no matter how rich in content, rare, or valuable—are worth little unless they are imaginatively and intelligently deployed on behalf of the museum's mission, and visitors are welcomed enthusiastically into its world. This sounds so obvious. Yet if we compare the resources spent on developing the collections to those spent on developing the staff and volunteers, the need for a much-enhanced level of "care" for the museum's human assets becomes even more obvious.

Most museums operate with two distinct categories of personnel: the paid and the unpaid members of its staff. Each is extremely important to the success of the museum, and their performance matters. It is important to keep in mind that the public sees no difference between these groups; each, for better or worse, represents the museum, but their duties and rewards are distinctly different. Let's take a look at each of these groups separately:

PAID STAFF: The paid staff is an essential museum asset. If the board is lucky, they are well trained in their subject areas, deeply committed to the institution, and tireless in their efforts to realize the museum's ambition. It is the job of the CEO to ensure that they are led, managed, mentored, and monitored. Communication between CEO and staff is extremely important because nothing can alienate a staff more quickly than to be surprised by something that is happening in their own museum. The CEO is responsible for the annual evaluations of senior staff and, in a general sense, for their care and feeding. But it is the board's responsibility to ensure that this is happening. The board does the CEO no favor if trustees are uninterested in the institution's investment in staff development or fail to ensure that staff members are informed and consulted, when appropriate, on important museum issues. To be sure, the level and type of investment in the staff will depend on the needs and resources available. However, the board should know that staff development is an essential element of improving museum performance and that the resources and time necessary to accomplish it are just as real a priority as collections care and educational programs.

UNPAID STAFF: From our perspective, museum volunteers—docents, receptionists, clerical staff, curatorial assistants—should be considered unpaid staff and part of the museum's regular workforce. Volunteers often have more contact with the public than anyone else in the museum, and the institution may well be judged by the quality of its volunteers—they meet, they greet and they inform. Most volunteers approach their work responsibly and see volunteering as more than just "something to fill up the day." They get great pleasure by helping the museum in its work. Nevertheless, museum volunteers must have clear and written job descriptions and performance expectations, similar to those for paid staff.

At least three-quarters of the museums we have visited or worked for have neither training nor written expectations for their volunteers. No one wants to take the time. The volunteers often are thought of as second-class citizens and treated accordingly. We have found it, frankly, embarrassing. To be sure, some volunteers are garrulous, some are crotchety with visitors, some *are* filling up the day; and museums should have standard procedures for dealing with these types of situations. But most volunteers provide an essential service—free of charge—extending the reach of the museum and its ability to serve the public. If the museum does not include volunteers in its family, they often form their own pressure groups, united too often in their grievances rather than in support for the institution.

Board members would be well served to get to know some of their museums' best and most active volunteers, who will have great insight into the institution and its visitors. They know what the visitors like and don't like better than anyone, and they'll be glad to tell you all about it. For board members to provide this kind of listening post for the museum is not micromanagement but good stewardship of resources.

Both categories of museum personnel are essential to the institution's success in the fullest sense, and the board has an important role to play in ensuring that:

- paid staff are compensated (both in salary and benefits) at a level and in a way that encourages continued loyalty and high performance;
- opportunities exist for the development of professional skills and experience and that, when possible, there are opportunities for advancement for both paid and unpaid staff;
- staff (both paid and unpaid) know their job duties and expectations and understand that performance evaluations, accompanied by constructive feedback, will be conducted regularly;
- that staff and volunteer handbooks, or similar documents, clearly define the responsibilities of staff and volunteers to the museum and the responsibilities that the museum has to them, particularly regarding such things as (for paid staff) vacation, sick leave, and benefits;
- that there are mechanisms for recognizing and celebrating the role of staff (paid and unpaid) in improving the performance of the museum.

If these things do not exist, it is the board's job to make sure they are put in place.

MONITORING MUSEUM PERFORMANCE

There is a feeling among museums and many other nonprofits that since the "bottom-line" measure of their work is a greater aesthetic sense, or increasing knowledge, or fostering better understanding, measuring progress and performance toward such an uncertain and imprecise end is impossible. Difficult, we would say, but not impossible, and certainly no excuse for not trying to find some key indicators to help board and staff measure the museum's performance. In thinking about measuring performance the board should keep in mind that only the most important things should be measured, and that what you decide to measure will have a large role in shaping the museum's behavior. If attendance is considered a key performance indicator, that sends out an explicit and implicit message—programs and activities that drive attendance are important. If the degree to which the museum is used by teachers to develop curriculum materials is measured, the message will be that this is an important activity, and the museum will shift its emphasis in this direction.

It is no different in the for-profit world. In a memoir about his years at General Electric, former CEO Jack Welch relates a conversation about measurement. He was questioning one of his senior executives about a dramatic decline in profits for the quarter, saying, "What the hell happened here? The response was: "Well, we had a fourth-quarter sales contest and everyone did a great job." Welch asked "Where's the margin?" The answer, "We didn't ask for margin." This little story shows that what you ask for is what you get; therefore, what you ask for is important. If a museum wants to increase its attendance, it will be more responsive to the needs of its audiences. If it wants to enhance its scholarly representation, it will be more responsive to the needs of scholars. But if it goes too far in either direction, it may lose an important constituent group. So, be careful about what you ask for and know why you have selected a particular focus. And if you are surprise or dismayed by the results, re-examine your focus.

As Joan Magretta writes in *What Management Is: How It Works and Why It is Everyone's Business* (Free Press, 2002):

> Museums used to see themselves as cultural custodians, repositories for conserving valuable objects. Given that mission, the contents of the institution's collection and the value of its holdings might be the appropriate measures of performance. Today, however, most

museums have a radically different mission. Now, most see themselves as cultural advocates, expanding the audience for inspiration, beauty, and taste. However, cultural advocacy can take many forms, and how success is defined will affect the behavior of the museum staff. If expanding the audience is the primary objective, the focus will be on increasing the number of visitors, which will encourage curators to create shows that are aimed very broadly. If the goal is building a loyal clientele of genuine patrons you might track the frequency of visits (the museum's version of repeat sales) or the number of museum memberships sold. Defining performance in this way makes the objective clear to everyone.

It is essential that the board, working in concert with the CEO and senior staff, develop a series of key measures of success that will provide a continuing report card of museum performance. We recognize that this is not easy. The outcomes of museum work—such as inspiration, growth in one's aesthetic sense, the gaining of new knowledge and awareness, the grasp of the importance of science—often are gained in subtle ways and over a long period of time. Yet this is no reason not to try. Certainly, existing measures, such as attendance, revenue, and annual contributions, can continue to be used since they track very basic and important things. For example, a museum whose attendance, revenue, and contribution numbers are going down is most probably in trouble. But measuring museum performance will take the board firmly back to the importance of mission. It is the clarity and focus of mission that, more than anything else, will help the board and staff. For it is only by knowing what the museum does, as well as the outcome and value of what it does, that the museum can truly attempt to measure what is most important.

The board's role is to ensure:

- that the museum has a program that measures the most important outcomes of its work;
- that the performance measures are regularly reviewed;
- that the outcome of the review of performance measures is used to change and improve museum performance.

CONNECTING WITH THE COMMUNITY

If the museum is to be a success, the board must serve as a constant link between the institution and its community. The board should function as a trustworthy source of information and insight by communicating the museum's importance to the community and taking unmediated feedback from the community to the museum. If the board has selected its members carefully, they will be representative of the community and probably heavily involved in other community activities. As such, they usually will be in a better position to gauge the museum's standing than will the CEO, whose identity always will be closely connected to the museum, thus hindering candid feedback. For this reason, it is essential that board members work hard to listen as well as talk, and take the community's perceptions and comments, as well as the insights gained, back to the museum. There, they can be assessed by the appropriate staff or other trustees and acted upon if necessary. While many museum CEOs and staff may see this as an intrusion into their work, and perhaps even a threat, it is an important board responsibility. If the CEO and the board have developed the partnership relationship essential to the effective running of the museum, such information and feedback should be seen as an important service provided by the board.

It is also important for the board to ensure that the museum has a systematic method of listening to its audiences. At larger museums, which can afford to carry out regular surveys or interviews with museum users, this task often is accomplished by paid specialists. However smaller museums have an advantage because their volunteers or staff often are able to solicit comments directly from visitors about their museum experiences. While the results are not as statistically valid as those from a more formal survey, think about what would happen if each day a significant number of visitors was asked three simple questions: What did you enjoy the most? What did you enjoy the least? What can we do to make your visit more enjoyable? The cumulative result of the answers to this question alone could yield a rich source of information for improving museum performance.

As we discussed earlier, one of the biggest changes in museums is their renewed focus on service to the community. To carry out that responsibility, the board must:

- ensure that trustees feel that they have the necessary information for communicating effectively about the "case" for the museum and its continuing importance to their peers in the community;

- ensure that each board member acts as a sensitive listening post on behalf of the museum and that the community's ideas, perceptions, or feelings are brought back to the museum;

- ensure that the museum has a program that actively requests feedback from its audiences about their experiences with the museum and uses that feedback in a way that improves museum performance.

SUMMARY

If you were to lay the pages of this chapter out on the floor or on a large table, and compare the amount of space devoted to the various issues, you would find that the longest sections are about finding and hiring a good CEO and the relationships between the CEO and the board chair and the board of trustees. This is not to suggest that stewardship of the museum's assets and financial resources, monitoring performance, and providing connectivity to the community are less important. All of these are fundamental responsibilities of any museum board of trustees. But the hiring of, and the relationship with, the museum's CEO is not just a multifaceted issue, it is one of the board's most important responsibilities. Others will help make sure that the museum's assets are well cared for and that its finances are in order; others will keep an eye on museum performance and spend time in the community, talking and listening. In these areas, the board of trustees works in concert with the CEO and staff and, sometimes, with paid consultants. But the selection of the CEO is the board's responsibility alone, and it is critically important.

Enough has been said about the actual process of selection, evaluation, and relationship building. While we also have said that the search for, and care and feeding of, the museum's CEO is a time-consuming process, we may not have emphasized enough how important it is to take the time to do it right—no matter what. Trusteeship is a voluntary activity, and all trustees have many other obligations in their lives. But the selection of the museum's CEO should be at the top of the list. The CEO will set the professional tone of the museum, be responsible for the psychological environment in which the staff work, hire and fire the museum's staff, manage its finances and assets, and represent the museum in the community. While the board of trustees is the museum in a legal and moral sense, the CEO is the museum in a professional sense. His skills will guide the museum and the board to success or, if unchecked, failure. There is no substitute for being thorough, patient, and relentless in attracting, hiring, evaluating, and keeping a good CEO.

CHAPTER 4

Recruiting Good Trustees and More

NOW THAT WE HAVE TALKED IN SOME DETAIL about trustees in general and, most important, the role of the board in improving museum performance, we will shift our focus slightly to more specific and practical matters: how to ensure that the museum has a good board and that each trustee is able to fulfill his potential, both as an individual board member and as part of a successful board.

On the following pages, we will detail the basic steps to finding, recruiting, inviting, and orienting new trustees to the work of the board and museum service. The type of trustee each museum is looking for will be different, depending upon the institution's focus and needs. But there are some generic features of good board members as well as basic components to the recruitment process for the board to consider. This is, in essence, a "how-to" chapter.

It may seem that our emphasis on what the board and the museum can "get" from a board trustee is horribly insensitive; are trustees to be *used*? Yes, we would say, absolutely, with only one condition—that the courtship be honest. That will ensure that the new trustee understands and embraces his role and is willingly used, thus playing an important contributory, not sacrificial, part in the strengthening of the museum.

Certainly a board must make membership in its body attractive, but it can do that best by ensuring that all of its members are people with a sincere interest in the institution, who understand the museum's mission and vision and are enthusiastic about supporting its work. The museum's visible success will be the payoff. The board must look for what it can get from a trustee, just as potential trustees will look for something important to contribute to; the very real joys of board service come from involvement in something worthwhile.

THE BASICS

Before we begin to talk specifically about adding new trustees to the board, we need to emphasize three things that should already be in place:

- The museum's staff, CEO, and board of trustees must be in complete agreement on the museum's mission and vision for the future as well as its direction, plans, and priorities.
- The trustees should conduct an analysis of the current composition of the board, looking for areas in which professional or technical skills are needed; personal assets, including wealth and contacts; representations of the community's diversity; and a variety of perspectives and ideas.
- Before any new members are added, the trustees should conduct an analysis to ensure that the board is the right size for the museum.

Let's look at these three issues in order:

Mission, Vision, and Plan

No museum can operate effectively without a mission, a vision for the future, and a plan for getting there. And no board can recruit unless it can articulate the museum's mission and believes wholeheartedly in the value of the services that the museum provides—that is where its enthusiasm comes from. Trustees should be able to list the museum's priorities without hesitation as well as describe how the board fulfills its function as a governing body. In short, the board member must have an enthusiastic answer for the "so what?" question with as much detail as a listener can bear.

Only when the museum's staff and trustees agree on the museum's mission, vision and plan will the board be able to recruit effectively. Trustees must know and be able to articulate:

- what the museum is about and whom it serves
- why this focus is important and to whom
- what value the museum brings to the community
- what the museum projects as its optimal future development and why
- what the current priorities are
- how the museum will achieve those priorities

Without these fundamentals in place, it will be difficult to select board members who can make a substantial contribution; in fact, it will be hard to have a real conversation with them. The recruiting board must be able to articulate why the museum is important to the community, region, state, or nation, and describe in detail the board's place in helping to achieve the museum's mission and vision.

Board Composition

The board must work to match trustee talents, skills, and energies to the needs of the museum. For example, suppose that the architectural expertise that was so necessary a few years ago when the museum was building (perhaps) its new wing is no longer particularly important. Instead experienced and capable fund-raising assistance and connections within local, state, and/or federal government are the new pressing needs. Or maybe there is a large ethnic population in the museum's community that is not represented on the board. Once the gaps have been identified, the board can focus its recruitment efforts on finding candidates who can fill those holes and whose presence will contribute to its strategic development.

Obviously a board is much more than a group of "representatives," each filling a needed slot. Nevertheless, any board is well advised to examine the issue of representation, not in the name of political or any other type of correctness, but because it makes sense. A richness of discussion will come only from a rich mix of people; a wealth of ideas will come only from a variety of perspectives and life experiences; and an exciting environment will come only from the interaction of different personalities. The need for a specific expertise is more quantifiable and somewhat easier to come by; the board simply has to understand where the museum is headed and the skills that will get it there.

Many boards have nominating or governance committees that analyze the current composition of the board and propose new members. But we have chosen to refer to the responsible party as the board itself, primarily because the ultimate responsibility for composition and performance rests with the board as a whole. No matter what the process, board members will have to vote on all proposed trustees; they will have to serve with all new trustees; and they will be judged as a body that includes the new trustees. Board development is an extremely important activity and, unless the board is too large and unwieldy to make it feasible, this activity should not be delegated to a smaller group. It is incumbent upon all board members to ensure that they are feathering their nest with the right kind of feathers.

Board Size

There is no generally accepted rule for the size of the board. Many museums have boards that exceed 40 board members; some have eight to 10, or even fewer. And, of course, others have everything in between. Which is the best, large or small? It depends.

Museums with very large boards generally delegate a great deal of the work to a much smaller executive committee. The executive committee can be more strategically focused than the larger group, and more flexible and nimble. Executive committee members are generally the most active members of the board, people who enjoy the process of being "insiders" and being able to "make things happen," and who are willing to give the extra time required. The downside of delegation to an executive committee is that others on the board may feel left out or that their service is not valued, and leave the board in frustration. Large boards often can and do divide into a number of standing committees to spread out the work and give all board members a sense of participation. And if they are any good at all, large boards are relatively effective at raising funds; if fund raising is the focus, the problem of having nothing to do evaporates.

Very small governing boards tend to model themselves after the boards of for-profit organizations; they are strategically focused and work closely with the CEO and other staff leadership. In many cases such boards have, because of their small size, a very small number of committees.

As the board sizes and structures its way of doing business, it should remember that large boards generally require more staff support and that every standing and special committee will require staff time to coordinate its activities. This is not an argument against large boards, just a reminder to board leadership to focus its efforts on what gets results. If a large board offers a wider diversity of opinion and more fund-raising opportunities, fine. But the cost will be unwieldiness, the time required to reach consensus on fundamental issues, and the administrative burden on the museum's staff. If a small board offers a better quality of board discussion and a quicker, more strategically focused organization, fine. But other groups will have to be created and mobilized to do some of the tasks that require more people, especially fund raising and special events.

The point is that the board is just a tool to improve museum performance. There is no right way or wrong way to organize, and no model for, the Ideal Board's structure. In fact, many successful organizations constantly tinker with their board structures and process as times and organizational priorities change. There is nothing wrong with this as long as the experimentation is purposeful and there is enough time to observe and evaluate the results of each change.

Let's assume that the basics are covered. The museum has an agreed-upon mission, vision, and plan; the composition of the current board has been examined and everyone agrees on the skills—personal and professional—that the board needs at this time; and the optimal size for the board has been determined. Let us further assume that there are some vacancies to fill. Where do you find the initial pool of candidates?

WHERE TO LOOK FOR NEW TRUSTEES

Where will the Ideal Board come from? A phrase from a child's nursery rhyme jumps to mind—"out of the everywhere into the now," or, less poetically, from almost anywhere. A little patience and a little creativity is all that is needed to find new trustees.

Examples of "prospecting" techniques abound; here is what one of our clients did that seemed to work particularly well. The "mine" was the daily newspaper, and they used it as their primary recruitment tool for everything—board members, volunteers, donors, advocates, and sympathetic legislators. They scanned the newspaper for the names of people who had distinguished themselves in some way; people who had moved to town to take on responsible positions; people who had been promoted; people who had won professional or civic awards; businesses that had been recognized for excellence. The only people who were not targeted were the obvious crooks and people who lived in other states or countries; aside from that, anyone was fair game. The "nugget" would be invited to lunch—no agenda, just a social, get-acquainted call with either the CEO or the board chair, depending upon the person. It wasn't long before the museum had a wide circle of influence in every sector of the community. Sometimes the cultivation period was long, sometimes it was short; sometimes these people ended up on the board and sometimes not; sometimes they gave money and sometimes not; sometimes they became friends and sometimes they had other interests. But always they were advocates in the community because the museum had sought them out. It was an excellent system for getting to know influential people and introducing them to the museum, its mission, programs, activities, and vision for the future. It required good staff work, scheduling, and follow-up, and a tireless CEO and board chair, but the payoff was great and more than worth the effort.

In general, boards will find new members by keeping their eyes open; by asking their friends, family, business associates, acquaintances in professional associations, and people in other museums or nonprofit organizations; and, yes, by reading the newspaper. In addition, the museum's CEO, who has a broad range of contacts as well as a sense of the board's personality and chemistry, can make an important contribution to the recruitment process. Staff, volunteers, ad hoc committees, community leaders, politicians, the chamber of commerce, convention and visitors bureau—all, if asked, will be able to supply names and suggestions that will broaden the board's reach; the list is almost endless. And one of the most interesting and useful things that will surface as you get deeper into the process of looking for new board members is that a name, or more than one, will be suggested two, three, even four times. When that happens, you are probably looking at the name of someone who would make an excellent trustee.

CRITERIA FOR NOMINATION

Before we go any farther, we must say that the board must take care not to become inbred. It is tempting to invite friends to join the board; they are a known commodity and they can be trusted. But can they, or will they, do the work? Is the museum one of their primary interests, or do they simply find it hard to turn down a friend? The Great Museum needs great trustees, and they should be selected for their interest in and commitment to the museum's mission and for the skills they can bring to the board—and not for anything else.

The process the board goes through in the selection of new board members is not all that different from the process the CEO goes through to select new staff, and it is equally important. A board must analyze the pool of potential new members critically and dispassionately: What do they bring to us? Will they fill a gap in the board's personality, talent, ability, and/or skills? Will we enjoy working with them? Will they provide honest and candid feedback? Will they be loyal? Will they take the job seriously? Will they take on the required level of responsibility and commitment? When the board selects its new members, it is selecting professional colleagues not friends, people who will help ensure the success of the museum to which all are committed.

While it is obvious that the needs of different museums will be different, there are a few basic criteria that should be considered when identifying prospective board members, no matter what the museum's focus is (see the chart on page 67). It will be important for the board to consider these and other questions specifically targeted to the museum's circumstances as it begins to talk about what kind of trustees are needed currently for the board and the museum.

Boards should involve the museum's CEO in the development of criteria as well as the recommendations of new board members; the CEO has as much to gain, or lose, from the selection of trustees as the board itself does. In addition, he will probably have the clearest grasp of the museum's short-term future needs.

Once the preliminary criteria have been developed, usually by a small working group, the entire board should have an opportunity to discuss them, make suggestions for additions or deletions to the list, and engage fully in the question of how to recruit the best trustees.

Then the board will be ready to consider the questions that will be asked of potential trustees during the interview stage. This is the courtship phase we referred to at the beginning of this chapter, the time in which honesty is not just the best policy, it is the only policy. Can this candidate provide what the board needs? It's a question recruiters will have to ask.

QUESTIONS TO ASK

Many boards falter in their well-intentioned attempts to help their museums because, during interviews with prospective trustees, they neither clarify the board's expectations nor the institution's true needs. A simple set of questions can guide the interview, ensure that all appropriate areas are covered, and set out the boards' expectations so that each person can make an informed decision about whether he wants to become a trustee. Again, all boards will differ in their needs and requirements, but a few fundamental questions might include:

- Do you serve on other boards and, if so, what priority will our museum have relative to your existing commitments?
- Do you think the museum is important to our community? Why?
- Will you be willing to participate in fund raising?
- Will you be willing to make an annual financial contribution to the museum?
- Will you be willing to contact your friends and acquaintances on behalf of the museum and its programs?
- Will you attend and actively participate in board meetings?
- Will you be willing to participate actively on committees?
- Will you be willing to attend museum special events, openings, educational programs, etc.?
- Do you have any special skills that might be useful to the board?
- Do you enjoy working as part of a team?

Obviously you will not sit across from a candidate and read off these questions. But these are important areas to probe, and the list ensures that nothing is left to chance. Some advance preparation will allow you to ask these questions with a little less formality but no less result—this is a "need-to-know" situation.

Again, the board must be sure that it is not just selecting people that board members already know or are comfortable with—unless, of course, they really would be the best choice for one of the limited number of spots on the Ideal Board. One of the most important services a member, new or old, can bring to any board is a different point of view and the willingness to express it. Many board problems, in fact, many museum problems, could be avoided if board members were only willing to challenge each other or staff seriously and ask the hard questions. What happens instead is that people with very different backgrounds or points of view often are not invited to join the board. It's just too messy to have to deal with them; there are too many unknowns and the board might lose "control." No one ever says this, of course, control still being exerted by the behavioral norms of the group; but to avoid the potential for discomfort, the board selects its "own kind" and the hard questions go unasked. A board can skate along this way for a while, but not for long. Not asking an important question is like skirting a land mine—you avoid the explosion but the mine is still there. Sooner or later something will trigger it. Far better for the trigger to be intentional, and sooner is much better than later.

CRITERIA FOR NOMINATION	1) Agree Strongly	2) Agree Somewhat	3) Disagree Somewhat	4) Disagree Strongly
a) Is this individual well known and respected in the community, someone who can provide new contacts for the museum?				
b) Does this person have the resources to make a significant gift to the museum, or to bring in others who can?				
c) Does the person have any special skills that will improve the effectiveness of the board, e.g., legal, marketing, or fund-raising expertise, or media connections?				
d) Will this individual bring a different and needed perspective to the board?				
e) Does the board represent the community the museum serves and, if not, will this individual help balance the board?				
f) Is the person a successful business person or an entrepreneur with creative, slightly off-beat ideas that would add a yeastiness to the board's discussions?				

First Approach

Once the criteria have been defined, some prospective trustees have been identified, and the interview questions have been approved, the board must find out whether the interest is mutual. This can be done in many ways but, unless the individual is well known to someone on the board, the simplest approach is by letter. The letter should be short and to the point and include enclosures of relevant museum material, such as mission and vision statements, a list of current board members, a calendar of events, annual report, Web-site information, and a list of what is expected from a board member. Don't drown potential trustees in information. If they are interested, you can always send more.

The letter below is just a start; its purpose is to give you the general idea, not to serve as a model:

> Dear Potential Board Member,
>
> You were recommended to us by _____ as a potential trustee for the Great Museum. As you probably already know, the Great Museum is well known for its _____ and _____. It plays an extremely important part in the life of our community [state, nation, world].
>
> I have enclosed some materials about the museum that I hope will be of interest to you. And I will call your office next week to see if we can meet at your convenience to talk about this in more detail.
>
> Best wishes,
> Great Museum Board Member

The Interview

At their first meeting, the candidate should hear why the board recruiter joined the museum board and why he thinks the museum is important; what special qualities the board thinks the candidate would bring; and what the candidate could add to the important work of the museum. The recruiter might also tell the candidate about the ways in which his own work on the board has been important, both personally and to the museum.

It is extremely important to discuss the board's expectations with the candidate at this time; if this is not done, there will be trouble down the road. Our experience has shown that many non-performing board members are simply uncomfortable with what they are being asked to do, had no idea they would be expected to do it (e.g., fund raising) when they joined the board, and see no reason to do something that they were not told was part of the job. And they are right. It would be like inviting someone to a party without telling him that he is responsible for the food. Then, when he arrives, a group of hungry and irritable people accuse him of wrecking the party by being too selfish to provide dinner. Not a good situation.

It also is of critical importance that the candidate's existing commitments to other boards be discussed openly at this time. All boards require the confidentiality of their members on such matters as personnel issues, board membership, special problems or opportunities, and fund-raising strategies. It may be that your candidate's loyalty to other organizations will preclude him from providing his best service at this time. If that is the case, you want to know it now. You must be assured that you will "get" the best that person can give. Especially in matters of fund raising, your board members' influence, contacts, and energy must not be diluted by their responsibility to any other organization. In addition, it should be made clear to any prospective trustee that much of the work of the board must be kept confidential. It all boils down to where you fall on the candidate's priority list. And it is important to know.

So, ask the important questions. By the time the interview has been concluded, the recruiting trustee should have ascertained whether the candidate meets the board's needs (the answer is probably "yes" if the board has followed its own recruitment criteria), and if he is interested in serving on the board. If he says no, do not be disappointed. It's better to know now than to fill one of the valuable spaces on the board with someone who is not particularly interested in the museum, does not want to do the work described, has other priorities, or has personal or professional obligations that would keep him from active participation. Boards are all too ready to gloss over the real work of the board for fear of losing attractive candidates. Lose them. They are not for you.

When the interview has concluded, those who choose to join the board should be able to answer the following questions in the context of the museum's mission, priorities, and ambition:

- What will be expected of me in a general sense?
- What distinctive skills, talents or experience do I bring to the museum?

• What is the best service I can perform for this museum?

The process of becoming a proactive rather than a reactive board member begins at the interview stage with the answers to the questions above and with what is essentially a call to service and a charge, not a social interaction.

Then, what you hope to hear is, "How soon can I start?"

THE FORMAL INVITATION

An invitation to join the museum's board is a significant event and should be treated as such by current trustees and the museum's CEO. We suggest that it not be done in writing, although a follow-up letter is most appropriate. Instead, a minimum of two board members and the CEO should invite the prospective trustee to lunch or dinner and tender the invitation in person. This should be a celebratory occasion; it is an important moment for both the board and the individual member. We believe that the solemnity with which this step is undertaken drives home the importance of the responsibility and privilege of board membership.

The usual alternative, a letter with the date of the first meeting and a few additional pamphlets or reports, does nothing to emphasize the value of the trustee's role. The position of trustee is either important or it is not. If it is, recruitment deserves attention at every stage. An analogy may drive the point home: If you spend a lot of time cultivating a donor for a contribution to a specific project, get the donation, thank the donor and then forget about him, you probably will miss a much larger contribution that time, trust, and attention would have made an almost sure thing. If you cultivate a prospective trustee, snag him, and then send him on an unaccompanied tour through an uncharted and confusing museum landscape, you may lose the deep commitment and involvement of a person who, with the proper care and attention, would have become one of your best board members.

During the course of the invitation lunch or dinner, include a brief reminder of the board's expectations to ensure the candidate understands and remembers what you talked about during the interview. When the formal letter of invitation is sent, it should be accompanied by a short memorandum detailing these expectations with a request that the new member agrees to and signs off on, something like the following:

- I will ensure that I am knowledgeable about the museum and its activities.
- I will be loyal to the museum and its board.
- I will read the materials that are sent to me and be prepared to discuss them.
- I will attend and participate in board and committee meetings.
- I will support the work of the museum's director and its staff.
- I will be an honest and thoughtful critic.
- I will participate in fund raising on behalf of the museum.
- I will make a personal financial contribution to the museum.
- I am aware that I am legally responsible for the activities of the museum.

New Board Member, Great Museum

This probably sounds like the Boy Scout pledge, but we can assure you that this is neither an elementary nor an unnecessary step. Lack of attention to the simple things can sink the mightiest ship.

Don't forget to provide the new trustee with a list of board members that includes a brief biography and, in the best of all worlds, a photograph of each. Do not assume that the new trustee still has, or can find, this piece of paper if it was sent to him as part of the initial contact. It is as important for the "freshmen" to know, and be able to recognize, the other members of the board as it is for them to know the museum's programs. Many new board members sit quietly for far too long, holding their thoughts and ideas because they are not able to address or respond to fellow board members by name and are uncomfortable asking, afraid of confusing one with another.

ORIENTATION

Before they attend their first board meeting, new trustees should have an orientation to the museum, its programs and activities, and its staff. The board can orient the new member to the board's role and responsibilities vis-à-vis the museum, usually through a mentoring process (described below). But formal orientation to the museum should be organized and conducted by the museum's director and appropriate staff, with a board member joining the group for lunch or at some other appropriate time during the process.

At a minimum, the new trustee should:

- have a private meeting with the CEO that details short-term challenges and opportunities
- meet with the museum's senior staff
- tour the public spaces
- visit the behind-the-scenes areas, especially the collections area, ideally in the company of the curator
- talk to the director of educational programs/exhibitions/activities/outreach—whoever is in charge of the museum's most public face
- meet with a volunteer
- be walked through the budget

The effectiveness of the orientation program is directly related to the amount of time it will take a new trustee to feel comfortable as part of the board team. If he has a clear sense of the museum and its public and behind-the-scenes activities, needs, budget, sources of income, challenges and opportunities, he will be able to join in board activity and discussion in a productive way right from the beginning. But if after the first, second, or even third board meeting, he is still trying to figure out what the museum does, or wants to do, and why, a lot of time will be wasted before he becomes effective, even minimally useful, on the board.

MENTORING

It is a good idea to assign one seasoned board member to act as a mentor to each new trustee. Such an arrangement provides continued reinforcement of the orientation materials and important issues and gives the new member a sympathetic ear that can listen to new ideas before they are laid out before the full board. The mentor can evaluate the new trustee's performance and help him adjust to the work of the board, his new responsibilities, and his new colleagues. The mentor is the new member's cheerleader and support, someone who can be asked the "stupidest" question, who wants nothing more than for the new trustee to become a valuable, involved, and contributing member of the board.

Many organizations see the value in mentoring, or at least say they do, and yet often no one will do it. When this is the case, the board should ask itself, Given that we all acknowledge the importance of mentoring:

- What makes it a difficult assignment?
- What do we gain by a mentoring program?
- What do we lose by not having one?
- *Do* we in fact believe that mentoring is important?
- Are we perhaps being a little bit lazy? Or insular? Or clubbish? Or selfish? Or shy?

Once you know the answers to these questions you should address them as a board and deal with them. Mentoring *is* important.

SUMMARY

Board development is as much a strategic issue as the direction of the museum itself. Appropriate selection, recruitment, orientation, and use of board members will contribute significantly to the ease or difficulty with which the museum is able to fulfill its potential and realize its future ambitions. It is a process that is critically important throughout the life of the organization, not just occasionally.

As we stressed earlier, it is obvious that the board must understand and agree with the museum's mission to be an effective advocate, fund raiser, steward, and governing body. It is important to convey an understanding of the mission to trustee candidates so that they can understand the museum's work before they are ever invited to join the board. The trick is to develop a board whose primary loyalty is to the organization. That can be achieved by selecting only those trustees who have a genuine interest in the museum and understand and agree with its mission, and by providing mentoring, support, and informal evaluation as the new trustee becomes used to the museum, the board, and the issues before him.

Now that the board has recruited trustees to carry forward its important work, it must ensure that its processes are in order, that its work takes place in a climate of openness and trust, and that the trustees, both new and old, will be able to make a significant contribution to the museum's success.

CHAPTER 5

Improving Board Performance

PEOPLE DECIDE TO JOIN A BOARD OF TRUSTEES for many reasons—some good, some bad. Service on a museum board gives a person a certain prestige within the community—an identity as someone with whom others wish to associate—and acquaintance with interesting people and activities. For some, it may be a nice addition to a resume or a way to make personal contacts with people who are influential within the community. For others, board membership may be primarily social, an opportunity to interact with like-minded people and be associated with an organization that is known and valued in the community. For these groups, regular attendance at meetings and a deep interest in the concerns and challenges of the museum are secondary. But for most, service on a museum board is an important volunteer activity that offers an opportunity to make a difference.

As we discussed in chapter 4, a good board doesn't just happen, it must be crafted carefully. Recruiting a good board begins with a real understanding of the museum's purpose, value, and audiences, as well as its plans, priorities, and needs. It also requires a self-examination designed to identify board strengths and weaknesses as they relate to the museum's current needs.

Once the board has recruited the right people to serve as trustees, it must work to keep them. Nothing will alienate a new trustee faster than a culture of hostility or passivity among the trustees, or board meetings that are long, boring, and about unimportant issues. If the board does its job right, new trustees will enter board service with energy and enthusiasm—they'll want to get on with it. It is up to the board to ensure that this happens.

For the purposes of this book, all boards are considered to be part of an established, rather than a start-up, organization. We would argue, however, that the steps for building a good board from the ground up are virtually the same as those for fine-tuning an existing board. In any case, board development is not something that is done once, but is a continual and continuing process. Times change, people change, and boards, too, must change. The basics of board development should never be far from the minds of current board members.

While the previous chapter dealt with the issue of selecting individual trustees, this chapter will focus on how to ensure the board's best performance. We could string together a wonderful philosophic essay to describe the evolution of a good board, but, in truth, what will make a board successful is 1) the recruitment, described in the previous chapter, and 2) the board's processes and rigorous attention to its own behavior, described in this chapter. It is the human being's impatience with detail that often hampers our ability to achieve all that is possible. A very wise trustee once said to us, "Sometimes you have to slow down in order to speed up." We, who usually race from pillar to post, could not agree more.

Let us look at a few of the details that influence the performance of the board. Our basic premise is that if you improve board processes, you will automatically improve board performance. Of course, that is not the same as saying that you will have achieved the Ideal Board. Naturally, a board, no matter how stellar its processes, is only as good as its members and leadership, its understanding of the museum and its priorities, and its understanding of the mission and how it is carried out. But organizing and disciplining the work of the board and the individual trustees will position your board to be the best that it can be—guaranteed.

We believe there are 10 areas trustees should consider when working to improve board performance: a mission for the board, the board meeting, keeping board members busy with real work, committees and task forces, the culture of the board, motivating the board and retaining good trustees, terms of service, succession planning, the exit interview, and evaluating the board's performance. These are discussed in detail below.

THE MISSION OF THE BOARD

While the magnet for all museum activities and for all staff and board activities should be the institution's mission, the board should have its own mission. A mission provides a rationale, and a charge for the board's work and may help prevent misunderstandings among trustees. Similar to a museum's mission statement, the board's mission should clarify three things:

- what the board does
- the outcome of that activity
- and the value of that activity

The development of a mission statement is an important activity for any organization and should not be undertaken lightly. What the board says in its mission has real meaning and should serve as a guide for the work of the trustees. Mission statements are not easy to write, and board members should not expect to develop the perfect one after a few hours of discussion. We suggest that development of a mission be on the agenda for three consecutive board meetings. (Unless, of course, the board only meets three or four times a year; in that case, a mission subcommittee should move the statement along more quickly.) At the first meeting, talk in general terms about the work of the board; at the second, begin to develop wording; and at the third, come to closure on the statement. A mission statement should not be long; a good guide for the board might be to say that the mission must fit on the back of a business card. To give you a head start, we'll show you what we mean:

> The mission of the Board of Trustees of the Great Museum is to work in partnership with the CEO and staff to provide a lasting legacy of careful planning; stewardship of the museum's finances and assets; and the financial resources needed to ensure that the museum will be able to fulfill its mission, achieve its vision, and continue to make a difference in people's lives.

Please do not create this statement in a hurry. The process by which you arrive at your mission and the discussions that lead to its development are almost as important as the mission itself.

THE BOARD MEETING

There are no hard and fast rules for how often a museum board should meet or for how long the meeting should last. In fact, the meeting schedules of museum boards are all over the map. Some boards meet only two or three times a year, others meet each month; some meet for two hours, some meet for two days—and everything over, under, around, and in-between. Frequency and duration, however, is far less important than what happens during the meeting.

The board meeting, sometimes impolitely called "the bored meeting," is where the real work of the trustees is carried out. That is where full discussion occurs, votes are taken, and courses of action approved. And yet, all too often, trustees either dread the thought of a board meeting—expecting an endless and boring series of reports—or look forward to a nice social get-together. In neither case is the individual trustee at fault. Rather, the blame lies at the door of the board chair and (to a lesser degree) the CEO, who plan and run the meeting.

We propose some check points to help ensure that your meetings are effective and productive. There will be some redundancy between these points and the board survey questions that follow, but we believe this issue to be of sufficient importance to allow for some repetition.

If attendance at board meetings is declining, it may be because the meetings don't deal with important issues, not everyone has a voice, or several strong members have taken over and intimidate others. Occasionally boards have to deal with the trustee who has a strong opinion on everything, leaving others wondering if the point they wish to make is worth staying in the boardroom for another two hours. This is obviously counterproductive to a good board meeting, and the board chair must deal with the guilty trustee and keep the meetings moving along.

The most common culprit, however, for putting the impatience factor into the red zone is the ubiquitous and completely senseless inclusion of a string of reports, from either board committees or staff, that require no action or discussion. These informational pieces should be sent to trustees before the meeting and discussed only if there is controversy or action needs to be taken. Self-indulgent staff and board members can take up to half a day giving reports; when it is finally time to discuss the serious issues, everyone is ready to bail out. While it seems, and is, reasonable to do away with verbal reports, don't expect to manage it without hearing some grumbling, at the very least, and/or veiled accusations about "an uninformed board." But we assume that those responsible for reports can write and that those responsible for knowing what's going on can read. To us, sometimes alone, this is a non-issue.

The following concerns should be on the minds of the CEO and board chair as they begin to plan a meeting:

- How do we ensure that the agenda and all supporting documents, including staff and committee reports, will be sent out at least two weeks in advance of the meeting?
- What are the important items that must be discussed at this meeting?
- What decisions will be needed at this meeting?

- How will we handle board members who do not come prepared?

- How will we ensure that everyone has a chance to speak?

- How long should this meeting last, and how can we keep to the schedule without abruptly cutting off discussion?

- What measures must we take to ensure that the minutes—with action items highlighted—are distributed within one week of the board meeting?

- Who will follow-up on board assignments to ensure that they have been completed?

These are important issues. While much of the background work of the board takes place in committees and ad hoc working groups, the only time decisions can be made is during the full board meeting. Trustees should look forward to the meeting, expect it to be stimulating and valuable, and arrive ready to give their best. A lively board discussion in which everyone participates, problems are solved, decisions are reached, and assignments are made will go a long way toward keeping the board engaged.

The best way for the chair to discover whether the trustees find the meetings effective is to ask them. We have found that a short survey following each board meeting can be very helpful. While, of course, you will want to design a document to suit your board's particular style and situation, we have found the survey on page 80 to be useful.

A post-meeting survey will help the museum's director and the board chair plan future meetings. The goal is to use the time of board members to the best advantage; the moment they feel their time is being wasted, they're gone.

Once the board is functioning smoothly, and dealing with the truly important rather than the somewhat interesting, it is not necessary to survey trustees more than once a year, probably during the annual board retreat. Until you are completely satisfied, however, that all trustees are fully engaged in the work of the board, it will be useful to check progress at every meeting.

Keeping Everybody Busy

Few boards are ever lucky enough to experience "down time," the time when most of the major directional issues have been addressed and the board is "coasting." But busy people seldom like to coast; it makes them nervous. They like to be engaged. It is the job of the board chair, working in partnership

POST-MEETING SURVEY OF THE BOARD	Yes	No
a) Did the meeting begin on time?		
b) Did you receive your agenda and supporting materials at least two weeks before the meeting?		
c) Did you receive your minutes (including action items) from the last meeting within a week of the meeting?		
d) Were there things on this agenda that you thought did not require board discussion? **Specify here:**		
e) Were there things that should have been on the agenda, but weren't? **Specify here:**		
f) Did the discussions involve genuine board responsibilities?		
g) Or did they slide into peripheral issues or micromanagement of staff work?		
h) Did you feel comfortable speaking up?		
i) Did you agree with the decisions made by the board today?		
j) If not, did you express your views?		
k) If you didn't express your views, why not? **Specify here:**		
l) Did the chair conduct the meeting effectively?		
m) Did the meeting end on time?		
n) Do you have any suggestions for improving board meetings? Write your comments on the back of this page.		

with the CEO, to make sure that no trustees will think, even for a moment, that they are wasting their time by serving on this board. Each trustee must be involved in the board's work in a real way and feel that his contribution makes a difference. Since we are writing about museum boards in general, we cannot address specific issues or opportunities that your institution may have. But we can suggest general ways in which trustees' time can be profitably spent on almost any board, including:

- accompanying the museum's CEO on fund-raising calls
- accompanying the museum's CEO on cultivation calls
- lobbying local, state, or federal legislators on behalf of the museum
- hosting breakfasts, lunches, or dinners for donors or other influential people who might support the museum
- providing special expertise to the solving of a particular problem
- providing mentoring to new board members
- identifying and recruiting new board members

Except for the final two bullets, all of these things require staff work and coordination. They are essential activities that can move the museum forward in real and significant ways. They only find their way into a section called "Keeping Everybody Busy" because often board members are not asked to do them, despite the fact that their participation is desired, even expected, and that they may be underutilized. Instead, the CEO, too hesitant to ask a board member to do anything "extra," either does it himself or lets it go.

Trustees are inadvertently set up for failure when they are not asked to perform tasks for which they are well suited, not expected to do anything beyond the ordinary, or not matched with activities that would be better accomplished with board intervention. Strangely, they are often held responsible for work they were never asked to do, work they probably didn't know needed to be done. It is unfair, but it is a fact of life. No one, especially the CEO, wants to cross the line into someone else's (especially the board chair's) "territory." But this genteel consideration for board members, which often results in staff complaints about the board, may be destructive in the end. The CEO should be encouraged to discuss, first with the board chair and later with the full board, the types of ongoing commitments trustees might make to the museum's routine work.

COMMITTEES AND TASK FORCES

For years, people have seen board committees as a way to engage the interest of board members and keep them committed to the museum. Yes and no. It all depends on the organization, the work to be done, and the type of board. With members of a good board, or any board with busy people, you will not get away with "busy work." Committees must fill a real organizational need, and they must do real work. Any decent board member will see through a useless committee assignment in a heartbeat.

Committees can keep an organization moving in the period between scheduled meetings of the board and allow trustees to use their time wisely. Whether an organization has standing or ad hoc committees depends on the work that needs to be done and whether it's a long- or a short-term project. Committees take care of background and preliminary work on issues of concern to the board and museum, gather information, and recommend policy and action for approval by the full group.

No matter what the board size, certain functions are usually best delegated to standing committees, which can devote the time and attention required. They generally include:

- Oversight of Finances: A committee (or, in the case of very large museums, committees) should be responsible for oversight of budget development and monitoring, adequacy of financial systems, the investment of museum funds, and the auditing of the museum's financial statements.

- Development: A committee should be responsible for working with museum staff and other trustees to raise the necessary financial resources for the museum.

- Board Development: If this work is not handled by the entire board, a committee should be responsible for working with staff leadership to identify, recruit, and orient new trustees, and with board leadership to develop an ongoing program of evaluation for individual trustees and the board as a whole.

Many museums have a plethora of other standing committees, covering such functions as collections, exhibits/educational programs, and buildings/ grounds, as well as an executive committee. The list can become very long. Whether such standing committees will be effective tools for improving museum performance will depend on the size, membership, resources, and stage of the institution's development.

In a small museum, the board may be called upon to take on or extend the skills that staff would be responsible for in a larger organization. In this case, the committees function as volunteers to support, in a practical sense, or even do some of the work of the staff. The use of trustee oversight committees for functional staff areas is highly questionable, however, especially in museums with skilled, experienced, and talented staff. While there is no question that board members and board committees can bring a common-sense perspective and special skills to the oversight of museum functions, sometimes that oversight leads to micromanagement and counterproductive second-guessing of the staff. That, in turn, can quickly debilitate the best staff and cause severe tensions and morale problems that all too often get out of hand.

In thinking about what committees to establish, the board must be able to answer the following questions:

- Do we need this committee and why?
- How will it improve museum, or board, performance?

If there is no ready and positive answer to these questions, then there is probably no need for the committee.

An alternative to the semi-permanent committee structure is the task force, a fluid body that has a specific charge and a specific deadline—at which time it goes out of business. Just as the work of the museum should change constantly, adapting to the needs of a changing society, the board also must be able to change and adapt. A multiplicity of issues will arise that may affect the museum's future and will need to be explored. Short-term ad hoc structures, such as task forces, can be delegated to investigate such issues and report on them to the board for discussion and decision. The advantage of this system is the mechanism for self-destruction that is built into the very nature of the work—a focused agenda, a limited time, and a particular product.

Trustees often volunteer enthusiastically for such working groups because the work is usually interesting, and they know that there will be an end to it and that something will happen as a result of their work. The urgency of dealing with an issue of importance to the future of the museum can be a great stimulus for good board members and can help spread the workload of the board.

BOARD CULTURE

Every board has a culture—or what we might call "the personality of the board."

Think about your own board for a moment. Is it stimulating and exciting; functional and efficient; dysfunctional and chaotic; or just not very interesting? Are board members lazy or are they high performers? Do all trustees participate in important board discussions or only a few? Is the board cliquish or culturally inclusive, reflecting the community that the museum serves? Do trustees engage in lively debate or passive acceptance? Do staff or board opinions dominate, or is there a productive exchange of ideas and good partnership between the two? These are all culture issues.

Sometimes it is hard for board members to figure out how the culture developed, but it is almost always instantly recognizable to an outside observer. There are extremely hard-working boards, lazy boards, contentious boards, boards that do not respect the staff, boards that do not respect each other, boards in which there is a lot of discussion about the issues, and boards in which there is virtually none. There are boards made up of rich people, poor people, working people, retired people, young people, old people, ethnic groups, local groups, statewide or national groups, and, occasionally and wonderfully, a board made up of all of these. There are boards that laugh and boards that are extremely serious in the performance of their duties. There are boards that consider themselves watchdogs and boards that consider themselves partners.

There are clearly as many different board cultures as there are boards; you want to be sure that your board has a positive and productive culture. For obvious reasons we celebrate the hard-working energetic boards whose work is aided by their positive culture; we are all the better for them. But for the purposes of this book we will discuss in detail how to deal with negative culture, since that is where the problems lie. If your board has a positive culture, you're doing just fine. But if not, beware.

Let's take a few examples of negative culture. These are situations you probably would notice immediately if visiting another board, but may scarcely notice in your own boardroom:

- a board that is dismissive of the work of the staff, considering itself equally competent

- a board that avoids fund raising, when it may be the most important work it has to do
- a board that tolerates long-winded discussion and is not scrupulous in the timing of its meetings
- a board in which most of the work is done by a small number of people, a clique if you will, who may comprise the executive committee or just be a group of friends
- a boardroom in which some of the people are afraid to voice their opinions, afraid of arousing the anger of volatile and strong board members
- a boardroom in which the chair or CEO cuts off discussion

As we have said before, there are as many examples of board culture as there are boards. What is important is to ensure that your board's culture—the way in which it routinely does its business—is a positive one in which the right work is being done in the right way. Simply reverse the above bulleted list to paint a picture of a positive culture at work:

- a board that expresses its appreciation for the work of the staff
- a board that works enthusiastically to raise money in support of the museum and its programs
- a board whose meetings begin and end on time, where important discussions take place in an efficient and professional manner
- a board in which all members are fully engaged in the work of the board
- a boardroom in which discussion is open, honest, lively, and professional; where differences of opinion are welcomed and engaged
- a boardroom in which the chair ensures that every board member has an equal opportunity to speak and be heard

It is difficult to explain how a negative culture becomes embedded in an organization. It often begins with one or two very strong personalities who want to control discussion, deal with the staff as little as possible, communicate nothing, and run the museum, in some cases by going around the CEO. Or sometimes it begins with a weak chair; little or no information before meetings, which consist solely of staff and committee reports; tolerated absences and lateness; and very little of significance accomplished. The interesting thing is that after the strong or weak trustees have left the board, and they do leave eventually, the culture remains as an unwelcome legacy. And people just accept it. Why?

We can boil it down to one word: honesty. Or maybe two words: honesty and courage. There is almost always at least one person in the room who knows when things have gone awry—whether it is the culture, which is a broad issue, or the unethical behavior of a particular board member, which is a much more specific one. More often than not that person remains silent. That is why bad things don't change; no one raises the flag; no one pushes; no one says, this isn't right. It is hard to change a culture and the "whistleblower" will not be universally loved, but it is important to encourage differences of opinion. While negative discussions or perceptions of the museum or its board must remain within the museum—trustees, above all others, must speak only positively of the institution to the outside world—they must be discussed openly by the board. Listening to other opinions is the only way to grow. Creating an atmosphere in which this can occur is primarily the responsibility of the board chair.

Remember the pledge that all board members sign when they come onto the board: "I will be an honest and thoughtful critic." This is valuable and important work; this is essential work. And we see it avoided time and again because of friendship, business relationships, fear of reaction, need for acceptance, loyalty, pity, patience, and laziness. Please remember: the board is not a club, it is not a network, it is not about the individual trustee or the collective group. The board is about the museum and its work, and it will be effective only to the degree that it is able to further that work in a positive way. Honesty and courage—quite a package. Sometimes uncomfortable, always important. How far will your museum get without it?

Motivating the Board and Retaining Good Board Members

A motivated board is active, interested, and involved and responds instinctively to the needs of the museum, providing resources, contacts, counsel, or strategic advice. It is much more rewarding to be a part of a motivated board than a social board, and it is a tremendous help to the museum and its CEO. If you have already attended to the aforementioned issues, you have addressed many of the things that keep board performance and trustee interest down.

Motivating a board is not very different from building a good board and developing a positive board culture. The productive members of any board want to move forward in support of the museum in an efficient and effective way and with as few distractions as possible. They are busy, successful people, and they didn't get where they are by wasting time—theirs or anyone else's.

Good trustees will become frustrated and leave if basic board responsibilities are not taken seriously. Such issues might include one or more of the following dynamics:

- problem trustees are not diffused or removed
- an incompetent CEO is not documented and disciplined
- the museum's finances or budget documents are not understandable
- the board does not take itself seriously as an important force in the life of the museum
- the staff does not take the board seriously as an important force in the life of the museum
- the museum's needs are not being addressed
- the board is lazy or self-indulgent

The ultimate motivating factor for a board, of course, and the thing that will help you retain your best trustees, is the museum's success—the health and value of the organization itself. Volunteers will put up with a lot, but you will lose them immediately with a lack of organization, a lack of purpose, or conflicting visions within the organization.

A few suggestions for ensuring a motivated board follow. We know that boards will have additional ideas as they begin to think about their own museums and the individual trustees with whom they share such an awesome (in the original sense of that word) responsibility.

- Get non-productive trustees off the board.
- Recruit good trustees to the board.
- Expect a lot of your fellow board members.
- Bring only important issues to the board for discussion.
- Make decisions and plan future action at board meetings.
- Ensure follow-up and accountability on all assigned tasks.
- Between meetings, use board members for their counsel and/or specific talents.
- Ensure staff follow-up and reporting back on trustee questions, suggestions, or work.

- Recognize each other for the good work that you all do.
- Establish good relations with the museum's staff.
- Establish an effective partnership with the museum's CEO.
- Always keep each other, and the staff, well informed
- Bring in experts to keep the board informed about issues that affect the museum (demographics, for example).
- Ensure that board meetings are scheduled one year out and that agendas and all materials are delivered well in advance of all board meetings.

If we were to highlight only one suggestion for keeping good trustees it would be: *do not waste their time*. As we have discussed already, the kind of people you want on your board are busy people. They will have little patience with small details or issues based on personality. They want to get the job done. Use their time well and on important things.

TERMS OF SERVICE

There is no one way to decide how long the terms of your board members should be. There are many types of museums, each with different needs and circumstances. Nevertheless a short discussion on this issue is in order.

We have seen boards whose terms are one year, boards whose terms are for life, and everything in between. And while there are advantages and disadvantages to whether board terms are long or short, our bias is toward longer terms. We are not suggesting that a board should change its one- or two-year term-limit rule without a lot of thought and serious discussion. But our experience persuades us that longer terms can develop more productive board trustees.

Some boards, and some CEOs, will shrink in horror at the thought of longer terms. Longer terms? How could you get a disruptive or non-productive member off the board? Many boards and CEOs long for the day when a problem child's term is up and breathe a sigh of relief when he leaves the board.

We do not believe that this type of thinking is productive. Of course, you can, and should, get bad board members off your board whenever it becomes necessary. It is your responsibility to develop the best board possible, and that means both careful selection of board members up front and "early retirement" of bad board members, if something was missed during the recruitment process. (See also chapter 6, "Handling Difficult Board Issues.")

In our experience, it is difficult trustees who keep many boards from opting for longer terms of service. That is a cop-out. Let's look at the pros and cons of longer terms of service for trustees, using, for the purposes of discussion, a four-year term with an optional renewal for an additional four years.

On the positive side:
- Trustees will understand thoroughly the museum and its issues.
- Trustees instinctively will know what the museum needs to succeed.
- Trustees will become comfortable with their role of supporting the museum in all ways.
- Trustees will feel a greater sense of investment and responsibility.
- Trustees will have an opportunity to grow with the museum.
- Trustees will develop a deeper partnership with the CEO.
- Trustee leadership will emerge and be obvious.
- Trustees will have a greater opportunity to make a significant impact on the museum.

On the negative side:
- Ineffective trustees will remain on the board for a longer period of time.
- Less turnover will mean fewer opportunities to attract good new trustees.

We have not intentionally stacked the deck in favor of longer terms; this is just how it appears to us. Many of you will have other ideas, and that is fine. As we have repeated throughout this book, every museum is different.

But from our perspective at least, we have answered the first negative issue: you can, and should, remove ineffective trustees from the board whenever it is necessary. We also would assert, in answer to number two, that a board will not constantly need new members if its current trustees are doing a good job. After all, this is not the Miss America pageant, where a new batch of pretty faces is required every year for whatever reason; this is a job in which experience counts. With the proper recruitment of trustees in place, and a process for disciplining rogue trustees, your board should be able to do an extraordinary job to support the Great Museum.

SUCCESSION

The constant motion of trustees on and off the board makes it hard to plan effectively for succession. Consistency and continuity are extremely important to the effective functioning of the board, however, and boards should think more about succession planning than they do. There is no value in the haphazard elective process that often brings in a new chair, and certainly none in the practice of a short term for the chair. How would boards like it if the museum's CEO left every year, or maybe every two years, the most common terms for board chairs? That kind of "herky-jerky" leadership makes it hard to take the museum where it needs and wants to go.

There are many ways in which boards select their chair:
- by competitive election
- by slate election
- by process (i.e., the vice chair becomes the new chair at the end of the current chair's term)
- by nomination (a particularly active board member stands out for reward)
- by default

The default election is by far the worst of these options; if a new chair is appointed by default, it means that no one wanted the job. That is tragic. The chair should be the most sought-after position on the board. Yes, there is a lot of work involved, but the rewards are great. No one is in a better position to help the museum and CEO make substantial moves forward or ensure that the board is well organized and works energetically and efficiently. The board chair has the authority and the responsibility to make things happen. If he is also good at delegation and has a good board, the task can be far less onerous.

The chairmanship of a museum board of trustees is a powerful leadership position and should not be given to someone who is unprepared. The leadership must be passed smoothly so the work of the board can go on without missing a beat, which argues for a formal succession process built into the procedures of the board. Moving from secretary/treasurer to vice chair to chair is one way to go, and many museums have elected to choose their chairs in this way. But it may not be the best way. Someone who is a good second-in-command may be hopeless in the seat where the buck stops; a good secretary/treasurer may have no interest in or talent for the chair's job.

A good board of trustees knows its membership well. While it is difficult for a museum board, whose members change over every few years, to grow leaders in the same way that a corporation can, every member can be on the lookout for potential leaders from the first day a new trustee appears on the board. It is the responsibility of the chair to develop leadership when he sees it; it is the responsibility of the other trustees to acknowledge and promote it.

But how can such a loose system work itself into a formal process? Good question. It probably can't. What is important is to acknowledge that the current process of succession does not work and that because, where it exists, it is rigidly formalized, a board may be stuck for several years with a chair who cannot do the job.

Let us reconsider the formalized succession process, with a difference. The current practice is to elect a slate of officers, each one considered appropriate for the position: The chair has leadership qualities. The secretary/treasurer has patience, and hopefully, although seldom, a financial background. And the vice chair is a nice person who will preside over meetings in the chair's absence. The current election practice does not require the vice chair to have the qualities to be chair, although he may, and it certainly doesn't assume such qualities in the secretary/treasurer. Nevertheless, these people routinely succeed to the chair position.

One option might be to continue with the traditional approach but formalize it at the vice-chair level. The secretary/treasurer is elected for his skills alone and not as part of the succession plan. In this scenario, when the board elects the vice chair, it knows that it is electing the future chair. Where this process has been formalized as a succession plan, it works quite well. It assumes that the trustees pay as much attention to the candidates for vice chair as they do to those for chair, and the election of the second officer becomes terribly important.

When the current chair's term is completed, the vice chair becomes the new chair. An election is held, and the board chooses a new vice chair, who eventually will *become the chair*. Once the process is in place, future elections are only for the positions of vice chair, with the understanding that this person will one day become chair, and secretary/treasurer, who is elected for needed, particularly financial, skills.

Indulge us for a moment in a short aside. The position of secretary/treasurer is notoriously misunderstood, often poorly executed, and seldom taken seriously. Many consider this extremely important position to be a throw-away office, a nice plum for a popular board member who wants to be an officer. The "secretary" part of the position is basically clerical. No one wants to do it and for good reason: a person taking detailed minutes is unable to participate fully in board discussions. The "treasurer" part of the job is of critical importance and requires specialized skills on which the board should insist. The two pieces of the job are completely incompatible.

We suggest that boards either hire someone or ask a member of the museum's clerical staff to take minutes. Issues of confidentiality would have to be considered, of course, and the minutes would have to be read carefully to ensure they convey a true sense of the meeting. But it is a far more rational approach than removing, in effect, a productive board member from full participation in discussions and diluting an important financial oversight role.

EXIT INTERVIEWS

Under no circumstances should you miss the opportunity to interview board members when they leave the board, whether they are leaving because their term is up, for personal or professional reasons, or they are being removed from the board. The exit interview will provide you with invaluable information that will help ensure that the board is operating to its potential. You might ask the following questions, or something very like them: Refer to the chart?

The collegial niceties that may have guided trustees' lack of involvement or criticism of board processes will become less important after they leave the board. A retiring, resigning, or fired board member may have a great deal to say, which, because of board culture or his own personality, was difficult to say before. Take advantage of this opportunity; the exit interview should be an ongoing activity of the board, closely associated with board development.

It also will provide you with an opportunity to encourage the trustees' continued involvement in the museum. Few museum boards have an active alumni group, and we believe that this is a great mistake. Former board members should be considered a part of the museum family; kept informed of museum activities by newsletter or personal contact; and involved in the

EXIT INTERVIEW QUESTIONS

a) Were you adequately prepared for board service?

b) How might we improve new member orientation and preparation?

c) What were the best moments of your board service?

d) What were the worst moments of your board service?

e) During your tenure, did you feel that the board lived up to its obligations to the museum? If not, why not?

f) What was the most important thing the board accomplished during your tenure?

g) In your opinion, has the board missed any significant opportunities for service to the museum? If so, please specify.

h) What suggestions do you have for improving the board?

actual work of the board, when appropriate. A great deal of time and effort is, or should be, expended for every trustee, from the moment he is identified as a potential candidate to the time he leaves the board. It goes against common sense to let all that experience drift away.

EVALUATING BOARD PERFORMANCE

Every board, from the smallest to the largest, from the newest to the most sophisticated, should evaluate its own performance annually. This is something few boards actually do. Trustees know that they are required to review the museum's director annually, based on a set of agreed-upon objectives for the year, and examine the performance and progress of the museum. And, for the most part, they are eager to do this.

Many boards, however, are reluctant to establish goals for themselves, analyze their own performance, and look for areas that could be improved. The idea that the museum's director and others outside the organization might give a candid assessment of its service to the museum seems to strike terror into the collective heart of even the most seasoned board. But if the annual review of the museum director is an opportunity for an honest exchange of ideas, an opportunity to learn and grow, why would such a review be a less significant opportunity for the growth of the board?

Due to this book's general nature, we cannot suggest specific performance measures for your institution. But some general ideas may help you design a board evaluation instrument, something, perhaps, similar to the one on pages 96-98.

Obviously, if the answer to any of the form's first 13 questions is "1" or "2," the board should work to remedy the situation immediately.

<hr>

SUMMARY

Service on a museum's board of trustees is a privilege that carries great responsibility. It provides an opportunity to make a real difference to the museum, to the people who use the museum, to the community in which the museum is located, and—if the board and staff are truly successful in developing an innovative and engaging museum experience—to the museum field.

The people who agree to serve on museum boards of trustees generally have a deep sense of civic and cultural responsibility; they understand and value the trust that is given to them and begin their tenure willing and eager to serve. But all too often this eagerness turns to disappointment. New trustees become disillusioned as the real culture of the board is revealed, and it becomes apparent that their vision of service will not be a reality. Some choose to leave the board and use their talents in other ways; some stay on, frustrated but accepting, until their terms end. In neither case do these people stay involved with the museum after they leave the board.

It is the responsibility of all trustees to ensure that this description does not represent their board. In this chapter we have discussed some of the processes trustees and CEOs might use to keep their boards engaged. Our basic message is to use the time of the trustees wisely and well, but, above all, to use it. Trustees have agreed to serve; let them serve.

In the coming chapters, we will discuss problems that many boards have as well as how to recognize and handle them. But we believe that the issues discussed in this chapter are crucial to the effective functioning of any board. We encourage you to evaluate board performance and individual member performance on an annual basis. It is the only way to know whether the board's service to the museum is organized and efficient, and, more important, whether or not it is valuable to the museum and its CEO. That requires an act of faith on the part of the CEO and the board, but without trust between these two parties, not much will happen. Given that there is trust, an open and honest evaluation of the board's performance will be extremely helpful to the board. If you haven't conducted one recently, we urge you to begin to plan for it today.

Trustees expect the CEO to get the best out of the staff; the CEO should expect the best from the trustees. And the trustees should expect the best of themselves.

Evaluating the Board

Rate both "yourself" and "the board" from 1-5, with 5 being highest.

Considerations	Excellent		Average		Needs Improvement		Not Applicable	
	Self	Board	Self	Board	Self	Board	Self	Board
1. Board make-up is appropriately representative of its community								
2. Board make-up is appropriate for getting the job done								
3. Board understands museum's mission and programs								
4. Board has productive relationship with museum's director and staff								
5. Board reviews budget and finances regularly								
6. Board is actively involved in fund raising								
7. Board members contribute financially to the museum								
8. Board regularly evaluates the CEO								

Rate both "yourself" and "the board" from 1-5, with 5 being highest.

Considerations	Excellent		Average		Needs Improvement		Not Applicable	
	Self	Board	Self	Board	Self	Board	Self	Board
9. Board has recent by-laws, policies and procedures, and guidelines for recruiting new members								
10. Board ensures museum's goals are being addressed								
11. Board meetings address important issues, and board members arrive prepared to discuss them								
12. Board discussions are conducted in an atmosphere of open participation								
13. Board members are used well in between board meetings								

97

Evaluating the Board

14. Please list three areas in which you believe the board should focus its attention in the next year, and say why:

a.

b.

c.

15. Please list three areas in which improvement is necessary, and say why:

a.

b.

c.

CHAPTER 6

Handling Difficult Issues

MANY BOARDS OPERATE OVER, UNDER, AND AROUND problems that they know about. This will never do. We have selected a few of the most common to discuss with you in some detail:

- Conflicts of Interest
- The Founder
- Board Micromanagement of the Museum's CEO and/or Staff
- Staff Roles/Board Responsibility
- Problem Trustees
- When Board and Staff Skills Overlap
- More than One Board
- Poor CEO
- Poor Relationship with the CEO

The point we want to make is that the trustees' inability or unwillingness to put their own house in order will harm the museum and diminish the board's credibility both inside and outside the organization. No board can function at maximum efficiency if it is constrained by internal problems. And if it does not deal with its problems, its best members will walk away in frustration.

In chapter 2 we discussed the board's responsibility for its own performance, and in chapters 4 and 5 we provided ways for the board to recruit, orient, and mentor good trustees and improve its processes so that it might perform in an effective and professional manner. We believe that board development and paying attention to board performance in a systematic and formalized manner is a fundamental duty of the board. Without a good board, service to the museum (which is the most fundamental duty) cannot be achieved. An unsophisticated board or a board of trustees that is well intentioned but disorganized will not help the museum much, but it won't hurt it. A dysfunctional board or a board with dysfunctional members can cause great harm to the museum not only in missed opportunities, but in serious image problems within the community. A lack of trust in the museum will result in significantly lower contributions, unwelcome media attention, and a climate that makes it hard for the board to attract good trustees and for the museum to regain its lost credibility.

Most board members know this instinctively, and yet boards across the country are operating at less than maximum efficiency or worse. Brave CEOs bring the issues to the board chair's attention and still there is no action. Sometimes the CEO is chastised for crossing the line between board and staff roles; more frequently he is ignored.

There are many reasons for a board's refusal to deal with its problems or, even worse, to deny that there are problems. Some of these appear to be:

- the need to assert the authority and rights of the board, the "don't tell *us* what to do," defensive posture, when in fact the board may not know what to do
- an unwillingness to damage personal relationships by challenging unproductive behavior
- an unwillingness to confront a person of stature in the community or to take on someone with an explosive personality
- an unwillingness to confront a person who has done a great deal for the museum
- uncertainty about what the board's rights may be
- a reluctance to change board leadership because someone's feelings may get hurt
- a lack of clear procedures for dealing with board members
- an unwillingness to risk public scandal or media attention
- a reluctance to change museum leadership for personal reasons or because of the time involved in a search
- the board has not evaluated the CEO on a regular basis and is in no legal position to fire him

Any of these would be understandable to most of us, but none of them passes muster as a satisfactory excuse. Obviously a board cannot be heartless, but whatever the issue is, whether it is one of the above or something else, the decision should be based on what is best for the museum, not what is best for the individual trustee, the CEO, or even the board as a whole. Trustees always understand this in the abstract, but when there is a real issue with real people, it is much harder to act.

For the purposes of this book we have chosen to examine a few of the most serious problems. We offer suggestions about how a board might handle similar situations and encourage trustees to recognize that, as in the "Conflict of Interest" discussion, there will be issues endemic to any gathering of influential people that can cause problems but, with advance thought and planning, should not. In such cases we can suggest no magic greater than the use of common sense.

CONFLICTS OF INTEREST

If a board does all the right things to attract and recruit wise, influential, and hard-working board members, from time to time there will be conflicts between the interests of the museum and the financial or personal interests of individual board members. The only way a board can completely avoid actual or potential conflicts of interest is to assemble a board of unsuccessful, uninvolved, and uninfluential people. Such a board would be ethically and legally pure when it came to conflicts of interest, but whether it would be able to work effectively to create a successful museum is another matter.

There are many reasons, some of them quite good, why a board might elect a trustee with a known conflict of interest. For example, if a museum precludes a collector from its board, it undoubtedly will cut off important potential donations during the person's lifetime or bequests from his estate. If the CEO of a successful investment banking firm is on the board and the museum refuses to use his bank to manage its endowment, it may be doing itself a great disservice.

Conflicts of interest among a board of engaged and influential people are inevitable. The important issue is how the board deals with such conflicts. The answer lies in the duty of loyalty owed to the museum by each individual trustee and the board as a whole. The trustee may not compete with the object of his trusteeship, in this case, the museum, in any way that might be detrimental to the institution's interests, no matter how small the issue. Any conflict of interest between the museum and the trustee must be resolved to the museum's benefit.

The best way to deal with conflicts of interest between individual board members and the museum is through a policy of transparency and regular disclosure; sunlight remains the best disinfectant for most organizational transactions. First and perhaps foremost, the museum should have a simple and straightforward "Conflicts of Interest" statement, which each trustee fills out and signs annually and uses to disclose any actual or potential conflicts of interest that may exist. Such a statement should include not only business and personal conflicts but also such things as parallel collecting interests. It also should outline procedures individual trustees can use to exempt themselves from museum discussions and decisions that may benefit them or a business in which they have an interest. A very simple "Conflicts of Interest" statement might be similar to the following, although, of course, you will have to tailor it to your own needs:

Conflicts of Interest

Pursuant to the policy of the Great Museum, I understand that, as a trustee, I must disclose any possible conflicts of interest that may exist in connection with my service on the board.

Attached is a list of all entities that I know are currently engaged in transactions with the Great Museum and in which I (or a member of my immediate family) have an interest in one or more of the following capacities: director, trustee, owner, partner, or other significant role.

In the event that any matter comes before the Great Museum's board of trustees, or any museum committee of which I am a member, involving any entity in which I (or any member of my immediate family) have a conflicting interest, I will notify the board or the committee of the conflict and will refrain from voting on and/or influencing the other board members about the matter.

Signed and dated:_____

Large or complex museums with special conflict of interest issues should seek advice from legal counsel or research model conflict of interest statements. (See the "Suggested Resources" section at the end of this book.)

The board should review and discuss its "Conflicts of Interest" statement at least once a year. And individual trustees should disclose any new conflicts of interest immediately rather than wait for the normal disclosure and review process. Policies and procedures are only as good as the board that develops and uses them; if they are not taken seriously, the board will put itself at risk. There is nothing more damaging to an organization than a perception that it is untrustworthy. If there is even the slightest hint that there is self-dealing on the part of the board or that a trustee has worked for his own personal gain rather than the institution's best interests, the damage to the museum's relationship with its stakeholders could be catastrophic.

There may be circumstances in which a potential conflict of interest (or the perception of one) between a potential trustee and the museum is just too great a risk, and the board will decide not to invite that person to serve as a trustee. Just as difficult, but from a different perspective, is the dilemma of a board member who serves on too many boards. How can this person serve each organization without dividing his loyalty? Unfortunately too many trustees fall into this category.

Service on any board of trustees provides advantages that individuals might not otherwise have; contacts are made and business cards exchanged. The business of a banker or retail merchant who serves well and effectively on a board may be strengthened because of his personal credibility. Service on a museum board may improve an individual's standing in the community, which can't be bad for business. Many people even choose to serve on a board for these or similar reasons. The key is that if there is a conflict of interest around any transaction the museum makes—if there is ever a conflict between the museum's best interests and an individual board member's interests—the museum must always win.

The Founder

This situation is so well known it has its own name, Founder's Syndrome, which refers to a museum founder who interferes with the work of the board or staff, usually both. A variation on this theme may occur in an organization that once had an ineffective CEO, or several of them in a row, and the board had to step in to keep the place going. In either case, the latent problem surfaces as a real issue when a strong director is hired. For the purposes of this discussion, we will focus on the true Founder's Syndrome, realizing that similarly dysfunctional situations can arise from different circumstances.

Founder's Syndrome often rears its head shortly after the museum's first professional staff is hired; up until that time the founder probably has run the museum. Often the rationale, seldom articulated, behind a founder's interference and micromanagement is that since the museum owes its existence to the founder, in some undefined way it belongs to him, too. The founding ideas are usually sacrosanct, and because a founder may have contributed considerable financial resources to the museum or encouraged his friends to do so, he believes he owns not just the museum but the mission, vision and programs by which it is known to the public. Often the founder believes that he knows better than staff or other board members how the museum should be run. It was, after all, his idea; who else should determine its future? When reality does not match up to the original concept, the founder becomes angry and seeks to redirect the museum to his original plan, whether or not that plan is still viable. In the classic case of Founder's Syndrome, rigidity and control come up against and reject new ideas and new data, although that may not be immediately apparent.

Once a professional staff is hired, the museum begins to change and may move beyond the ability of its board, which has not changed, to provide what is needed for the institution's development. At this point, it is important to get good and experienced new trustees, and many new CEOs work hard to get some new blood onto the board. That, however, may cause even more problems. The founder continues to interfere, often backed by his friends on the board, preventing the museum from fulfilling its potential. New board members, unwilling to go along with the founder's plan, raise unwelcome issues and generally side with the museum's CEO. The moment "sides" develop, there is a potential for big problems and a split in the board, which usually results in acrimony, bad performance, bad publicity, and ultimately damage to the museum's reputation.

Let's look for a moment at how a museum and a clearly committed individual may have gotten themselves into this fix. Perhaps it went something like this:

1. Someone has a good idea and calls his friends to help develop it. A board is formed, and its volunteer members set up the organization and perform much of the work. They begin to raise money; if their idea is a museum, they may begin to raise a lot of money and possibly even look for collection materials. What they don't do is test the market or the donor community, and usually they have no professional guidance. They ask each other if the idea is viable, and they enthusiastically give their own time and money to make it a reality.

2. The first professional CEO is hired, and new members are added to the board. This is always an extremely difficult transition. If the CEO is any good at all, and we must assume that this group of advocates searched for the very best, he will begin to conceptualize the idea within a professional framework. The founder begins to get nervous as he sees the possibility that the founding idea may change. The new, larger board, taking its role as fund raiser seriously, begins building a case for support and, after testing it with the donor community, finds that there are holes in the case.

3. As the new CEO conducts market research, becomes familiar with the collection materials, and becomes known in his own right in the community, reality begins to set in. The CEO's willingness to explore other options to achieve the same end (a less expensive building, a Web-based organization, an entirely different location, a different slant on the material), is matched by a hardening of the founder's position.

4. Founding board members, also invested in the original idea, support the founder, who is often their friend. New board members may begin to question some of the original assumptions and favor the CEO's somewhat different approach. There is a danger now that the board may split, causing irreparable damage to the project's positive public image and a loss of interest and loss of donations. Sometimes the CEO is fired; less frequently the founder is eased off the board. No matter which of these unhappy scenarios plays out, it will be years before the idea can regain its lost credibility in either form.

Founders who sit on the boards of established museums can cause as much damage to the organization as the founder who is working to develop a new museum. Generally, these are respected if not beloved people who have given a great deal of money to the museum, and they often have friends on the board. This is one of the most difficult situations a CEO can face because, when conflicts arise, the issues quickly become personal. Founders seldom move with the times and, for reasons completely obscure to us and against all common sense, continually insist on having their own way. Board members that see this situation playing out in their own organization absolutely must do something about it, no matter how uncomfortable it may be, no matter if the founder is their own mother. We believe that boards really only change from within. and while there is a lot that staff can do to help, ultimately change and discipline is a peer-driven process.

BOARD MICROMANAGEMENT OF THE MUSEUM'S CEO AND/OR STAFF

We believe strongly that if the museum has a good CEO and a competent staff, selected on the basis of their credentials and experience, the board should let them do their jobs without interference. At the same time, it runs quite counter to common sense for staff to assume that the board should shed its skills, experience, and expertise at the door of the museum. The key is for board and staff to have the mutual respect to talk about issues and discuss problems immediately rather than allow them to escalate. Trustees should keep in mind that they may not know how a staff member feels about being called to task on a professional matter; any staff member who confronts a trustee is taking a risk that a board member confronting a staff member is not.

We refer board members back to one of their most important responsibilities—the hiring of the CEO. If the board has selected a person with appropriate qualifications, integrity, and energy, it must allow that person to do the job for which he was hired, that is, running the museum.

There are a number of reasons why this seemingly simple dictum is so often ignored, among them:

- Board committees often appear to give the board responsibility for the work of the staff, e.g., Collections Committee, Program Committee, Exhibition Committee, Special Events Committee.
- During difficult financial times, the board may have assumed some day-to-day responsibilities for the actual work of the museum; when the museum's finances improve they may be reluctant to return that responsibility to the staff.
- One or more members of the board may have worked for the museum in the past.
- The museum's former CEO may have been put on the board when he retired.
- The museum's founder may be on the board.
- Family members of the founder or an original donor may be on the board.
- Major donors may be on the board.
- Members of the board may have specialties in areas similar to those managed by staff.

If you look at this list carefully, you will see that each category represents one or more people with a vested interest in the continuation of their own legacy or recognition of their professional expertise rather than people whose primary loyalty is to the museum and whose sole agenda is the realization of the museum's mission. Clearly, this is not always the case and, in fact, many museums' most treasured trustees fall into one or the categories listed above. But such situations can go very wrong.

The board does a terrible disservice to the museum and its CEO if it allows any of the trustees to assert more privilege than is due them. Remember, the board is a unit; it may not think or deliberate as a unit, but when it acts, it acts as one. To preserve its own credibility, the board must discipline its own; social niceties have to give way to governance responsibilities.

An extreme but illustrative example is the board whose members included a financial wizard. Nothing the chief financial officer (CFO), a competent person, did for the museum was ever right. The wizard second-guessed every move and dismissed the CEO's requests that he play a less proactive role; not surprisingly, several CFOs left. Finally, when the CEO was unable to find a replacement, the wizard took the job *and* remained on the board. Now he had plenty to say about the CEO. Everyone knew it was inappropriate, but no one did anything about it. Where was "the board"?

STAFF ROLES/BOARD RESPONSIBILITY

For the purposes of discussion, we have singled out two areas—budget and programs—in which board interference may be justified. They come from our experience with many boards, although we add the caveat that such issues can arise in any area of the museum and are directly related to obvious board responsibilities:

- The board is the legal fiduciary and must be responsible for and take care of the museum's finances.
- The board is the museum's link to the community and must ensure that the museum's constituents are well and appropriately served.

Staff notoriously dislike board interference of any kind, and for the most part we wholeheartedly support their position. Nevertheless, as we have said and as staff must remember, ultimately the board is legally responsible for the museum's performance. A good board can provide oversight and partnership without crossing the line into micromanagement.

We have selected budget and programs for discussion because there is a tendency for boards to delegate too much authority in these areas. With the budget, it is because many board members consider themselves unqualified to examine the organization's finances critically. With the programs, it is because the staff often feels the board to be unqualified in this area.

The Budget

Many museums, particularly small to mid-sized organizations, have financial documents that are almost incomprehensible. Often the staff person in charge of the budget has been with the museum for a while, is competent and hard working, and has moved up in the ranks without formal training for the job of museum finance officer. That works fine for a while, but as the museum grows and its finances become more complex, the situation becomes less satisfactory. This is not to say that the staff member does not understand the museum's finances; he nearly always does. But he may not able to look at the budget strategically, project into the future, do cost-benefit analysis, or find the true cost of exhibitions and programs, including such ancillary expenses as staff time. He may have developed his own financial systems that are perfectly accurate but extremely difficult for others to read and understand. When they try to understand such financial statements, many board members believe that the fault is their own, and so they don't ask for help. That is a great mistake. There is usually at least one person on the board who is familiar with budgets and balance sheets—a banker, a businessman. These people should not only raise the flag, they should demand financial statements that are clear and give a picture of the museum over a period of several years. All board members need to understand these important documents; that is not micromanagement but just good sense.

If a board is working with less than clearly understandable financial statements, neither the trustees nor the museum is getting the most out of the process. It is for this reason that in chapter 5 we stressed a reconsideration of the role of secretary/treasurer of the board. The board member responsible for oversight of the museum's finances must understand them. All boards would be well served by having a member who is a skilled accountant or finance person, preferably serving as treasurer, or by having periodic private consultation on financial matters. This should not be left to the once-a-year audit, and board members should feel perfectly comfortable about asking questions about the budget.

The Programs

Few, if any, museum staff welcome board interference with programs; after all, that is the staff's particular area of expertise. Most museum employees have been professionally trained and are specialists in their field, so it is perfectly understandable that they do not want to be second-guessed by trustees who have neither the training nor an understanding of all of the issues. In general, our sympathy is with the staff. The danger, however, comes when staff automatically retreat behind their "professionalism" and reject perfectly good, common-sense advice to the detriment of the program and the museum

There are occasions when a board member should insert himself into the process and make recommendations about program topics, interpretation methods, and delivery of information—not the professional "stuff," but the common sense of it all. Since museums are notoriously jealous of their prerogative as "the expert," trustees need to be as alert to an inbred culture within the museum as they are to an inbred culture on the board itself.

If the trustee is a visitor to the museum and a consumer of its programs, as all trustees should be, he is far more likely to hear about the museum from other visitors, acquaintances, family members, and professional associates than is the staff. Trustees will know what works and what doesn't in a more personal way and, like the museum's other volunteers, they may be closer to the audiences than the staff. Attendance figures say a great deal about the museum's ability to reach its community with programs that give value to their lives. Trustee (and other volunteer) opinions and insights should be respected and considered by the professional staff. Trustees should raise the flag when they see something that does not seem to fit the museum's mission or audience, or when there is a missed opportunity. They have the right to do so and should certainly be listened to.

Many trustees come into their museums only for board meetings or for exhibition openings, which is a poor way to get a clear picture of the organization. The focus at board meetings is entirely different, and openings are primarily social occasions rather than opportunities to really look at an exhibition or much of anything else. Neither of those "visits" qualify as the kind of experience of the museum a trustee needs to provide his best counsel and service.

An example comes from an institution we came into contact with shortly after the Sept. 11, 2001, terrorist attacks. One department had scheduled an exhibit on Hollywood stars; another department wanted to change the schedule and put up an exhibit on Afghanistan, showing at a minimum where it was, as most museum-goers had no idea. The board did not interfere, the curator who had secured her place on the schedule would not relent, and the Hollywood show went forward for no reason other than it was planned. The museum missed a big opportunity to provide value to a community hungry for knowledge about a country that would have a large and continuing effect on all of us.

PROBLEM TRUSTEES

It is not unusual for a board to have one or more members who dominate the conversation, are hostile to other board members or the CEO, refuse to meet the board's expectations of performance, or are just plain difficult. If this is an ongoing problem, good board members will leave the board, often without citing a reason.

Board members can and should be fired if they do not contribute in a significant, positive way to the work of the board and the success of the museum. The board should understand that the problem trustee is taking up a space that could be filled by someone who has a greater commitment to the museum or who is willing to cede some of his individual autonomy to become a productive trustee. Admittedly, the dismissal of a board member is politically and socially charged, and before the board does anything it must weigh the disadvantages against the advantages of removing a trustee. But it must act, unpleasant though it may be. If someone is hampering the work of the board, it must get rid of him.

The ultimate responsibility falls to the board chair, of course, but he should not consider such a move without first having an open discussion with the museum's CEO. If both agree that there is a problem, then the chair should talk to the board member in question, advising him that his behavior must change or he will be removed from the board. If the person does not change and continues to disrupt meetings, the work of the board, or the museum's positive image in any way, the full board should be polled. If a majority of the trustees agree, the person should be fired. It is the duty of the board chair to handle the difficult exit interview.

Of course, this is much easier said than done. Trustees are sensitive to each other's feelings and opinions. They often feel that they don't have the right to correct someone else, especially on the issue of personal behavior, since that person is not only a peer but probably a donor and certainly someone who is freely giving their time to the museum. Many boards just put up with behavior that in their own businesses or professional settings never would be tolerated. There, a disruptive employee, peer, or customer would have to be disciplined; to do otherwise would be bad for business. It is bad for the museum's business, too.

The easiest way to deal with such a situation is to prepare for it at the beginning, and here we go back to the board's foundation documents. There should be a process for removing unproductive trustees from the board, whether it is because they are unable to work as a part of a team, or do not attend board meetings, or for any other reason specific to the circumstances of the museum. Such a process should be written into the board's policies and procedures, incorporated into the orientation for new board members, and adhered to religiously. Usually boards have a procedure for removing someone who does not attend a certain number of meetings, but surprisingly few boards have a procedure for dealing with a trustee's inappropriate behavior. The board will make its own job easier if it develops a process for handling this sticky issue. In this way, board members will know in advance what is expected of them as well as the consequences for poor performance.

When Board and Staff Skills Overlap

This situation can arise in any museum where a strong and effective board, dedicated to the museum, interacts with a skilled and talented staff. Whether or not it is well handled depends on how the board sees its role. If the board sees itself as an overseer or watchdog, it will be on the lookout for errors, determined to ensure that the museum avoids mistakes before they happen. Clearly, most of these issues will be a matter of judgment and perspective. Nevertheless, the board member's point of view frequently will carry the day because of the uneven power relationship between board and staff. For this reason, trustees must be vigilant in monitoring their interactions with the staff, never assuming for themselves a prerogative that really belongs to the staff. Few bankers, lawyers, or business people would grab the scalpel out of a surgeon's hand and operate on a supine patient, but they may not hesitate a nanosecond before telling the museum's professional staff how to design an exhibit, even what the exhibit should be about.

The result of this is a breakdown in the partnership between board and staff. This is not to say, as we discussed above, that the trustees do not have a right to express their opinions or expect answers from the staff. Of course, they do. But they first must be sure that there is something at stake that might cause harm to the museum and, if that is the case, ensure that their "critique" is done with sensitivity and their questions do not sound combative. Otherwise the staff will see the interchange as an attack on their competence and professionalism and a lack of respect for their experience and training. The situation may escalate into a personal power struggle rather than a dialogue, one that either drives the staff member out the door or into a defensive posture in his future work, which of course prevents him from doing his best.

There are no magic bullets of policy or procedure that can prevent such a scenario. To say that a board member should not offer advice and counsel to a staff member when there is something important to be said and learned runs counter to good sense. But board members must exercise self-restraint when the issue relates to personal taste or individual philosophy; interfering with the work of the staff, except when there is a particular problem, is not a role of the board.

The only way that this difficult and yet crucially important issue can be addressed is by changing the philosophy that animates the board in its quest for improved museum performance. It goes back to our "new work of the board" discussion at the beginning of this book. In the old board/staff model the issue of who proposes and who disposes, who sets policy and who carries out policy, provides a clear division of power but adds no value to the museum's performance. In the future, the most successful organizations will be the ones that can figure out how to effectively share power and expertise and deliver it for the public good.

The museum cannot assemble and put to work a group of smart, talented, experienced, and influential trustees without expecting them to ask questions and demand results at every level of the organization. At the same time the museum cannot assemble a staff of smart, talented, and experienced staff members and not allow them to have the latitude to have their own successes and make their own mistakes. Even more important, the museum cannot expect the CEO to negotiate between board and staff because he surely will be ground up in the process.

So, what should you do?

The board has a serious responsibility to grow the talent and expertise the museum needs to do its work. It does this by selecting leadership, setting the boundaries, offering advice, and letting staff make and learn from their own mistakes. Working with sensitivity, board members can mentor staff in myriad ways that will grow their potential without necessarily creating the appearance or reality of micromanagement. Financial expertise and perspectives can be put forward in a way that is not threatening; board members can share "war stories" of their own failures or lessons learned in a way that does not negate staff experience or expertise. The issue is not power and control but partnership, and all those involved in pushing the museum's agenda forward must remember this and develop an environment of trust and candor.

More than One Board:

We have worked with museums that have one board; we have worked with museums that have two boards; and we have worked with one museum that has three boards. This may seem like an excess of riches and a disaster waiting to happen, but sometimes there are reasons for a museum to have more than one board. We dedicate this section to those of you who do.

Municipal- or state-owned museums generally have two boards: a (usually) advisory body, appointed by the funding agency, e.g., the governor or mayor's office, and a body that is incorporated as a 501(c)3 organization to provide private support (i.e., raise funds) for the museum. The situation is often complicated by the fact that the museum's CEO may report not to the boards, but to a public official. A museum that is part of a larger organization, such as a university, may have a similar structure.

While the situation described above may not be ideal, it is often perfectly functional. In fact when it works, the museum has double the human resources and double the advocates. But when it doesn't work, the museum and both boards have double the headaches; there are twice as many opportunities for conflict, for lack of communication and collaboration, for micromanagement, and for sending mixed messages to constituents, funders, and even staff. It can be, and often is, a terrible situation.

In our work we generally have found that the problems are less likely to be between the boards and the CEO and more likely to be between the boards themselves. This, of course, puts the CEO between the boards, an extremely uncomfortable place to be. Two boards serving the same institution are likely to be composed of peers who travel in the same social and, usually, political circles. Often they are reluctant to openly defy one another, but are quite willing to engage in parking-lot conversations about each other. The two groups eye one another warily. Usually the museum's board of trustees thinks of the other group, often called the Foundation or Society, as a service group with a sole task—to raise money. In this circumstance the museum's trustees often mirror the impatience generally associated with CEOs when the subject of board fund raising is raised. The trustees have absolved themselves of any responsibility for this important task; after all, it is in the foundation's job description. But they don't think the foundation is doing a very good job, and they always think that the foundation wants to be entirely too involved in the museum.

The foundation is aware of, and resents, how it is perceived. Foundation members believe that if they are expected to raise the money, they should have some involvement in the museum's planning process. That way they will understand from the beginning why a particular project is a priority, know the museum's long-range plans, and possibly even influence the museum's development. Without such knowledge how can they be expected to "sell" the museum and its programs? They must know more. "Outrageous!" say the museum trustees and, often, the CEO. "Makes perfect sense," say foundation members.

Recently, we participated in a foundation board meeting at which an architect presented plans for a major new exhibition with a price tag of just under $400,000. It was the first time the board members had seen or heard anything about the project beyond its name. They asked some very legitimate questions: What would be the museum's additional operating costs as a result of this new exhibition? Why was this particular exhibition a museum priority? What was the importance of the story it would tell, and why this one rather than another? How many people did the museum anticipate the exhibition would attract? How could the programs of the project be extended, perhaps through use of the Internet, to reach more people?

The foundation was not questioning the validity of the project; members simply were trying to get information they would need to "sell" it. The CEO was furious, the staff was angry, and the other board was annoyed that the foundation would trespass on what it saw as its territory. It was terribly disheartening, because the foundation's questions were perfectly reasonable.

Part of the problem was that the museum had spent so much time designing the exhibition that questions examining the "so what?" and the costs (beyond construction) had not been addressed. This should have been a partnership effort, with questions asked and addressed in the earliest stages of planning. But it wasn't and, sadly, this situation is not unusual.

Let's examine this psychology for just a moment and try to understand why the lines have been drawn so strongly. True, there are regulations that make it difficult for government-appointed boards of trustees to move as freely through the community as a board set up specifically for that purpose. But it's not that hard. Usually, appointed boards are made up of well-connected, politically active, influential individuals; who better to advocate on behalf of the museum? What a waste when they don't.

Foundation or Society boards also are composed of well-connected and influential members of the community. In the best of all possible worlds, they have either significant personal assets or access to others with significant personal assets. They are just as intelligent and just as committed as the trustees, and they bridle at serving as a banker for a potentially heedless client. They want a say in the museum.

The backgrounds of the people who serve on both types of boards are practically identical. They are often friends, neighbors, relatives; sometimes they even move back and forth between the boards. And yet, strangely, they take on the culture of whatever board they are on at the moment, never bridging the gap between the two. Both boards almost always work in an information vacuum: Trustees don't communicate important information about the museum to the foundation board, whose members may choose to raise money for their own favorite projects, rejecting the museum's priorities. And the CEO either lays low or, worse, manipulates the two boards so that no matter what happens, he looks good and they look bad.

The situation may be complicated by the fact that the trustees, who are politically appointed, may care less about the museum than the foundation members, who volunteer for the job because they love the institution. This is a serious and very real issue. The way political appointees are selected to a museum's board can cause problems. As we have stressed throughout this book, a great deal of the board's success rests on how trustees are selected in the first place. Whether they are patronage appointees or volunteers, it all boils down to the same thing—are they the right people for the job?

Earlier in this book we discussed in great detail how to get the right kind of board member and how to keep him interested. Regrettably, when the trustee is a political appointee, the system may break down entirely; his service on the museum's board may just be the straw he has drawn. Herein lies one of the biggest problems: foundation members, for whom service for the museum is usually a major interest, often look with skepticism at the museum's appointed trustees as they make decisions affecting an institution about which they may know little.

Obviously there are many, many politically appointed governing boards that do a fine job, and there are Foundation or Society boards that do not. We do not mean to suggest otherwise. But there are many museums operating now with two boards, at least one of which is not living up to its responsibility. What can be done? We suggest the following few steps at a minimum; you will know the specific measures needed for your particular museum:

- Make sure that there are criteria for membership on the board of trustees, whether it is politically appointed or not, and that government officials understand the importance of paying attention to those criteria when making appointments to the board.

- Make sure that expectations of trustees go beyond meeting attendance and providing oversight.

- Clarify at the outset what "oversight" means. Many politically appointed boards believe, and even say, that their job is to make sure the museum isn't doing anything wrong. They see themselves as the museum's watchdogs, presupposing that the museum needs a strong arm to keep it from doing something illegal, immoral, or stupid. We suggest that it would be more productive for board members to think themselves as "the museum's partners," with the underlying charge to help the institution be the best that it can possibly be.

- Define roles and responsibilities for both boards.

- Realize that the people who raise the money will want a say in how it is spent.

- Make sure that communication between the two boards and the museum's CEO is open and productive and that no one is surprised by anything.

- Foundation members should realize that while it is understandable, and should be acceptable, for them to be involved in discussions about the institution's direction and priorities, the museum trustees are the ones who are legally responsible.

- The foundation should be careful about refusing to support one of the museum's priorities. As we mentioned earlier, problems often develop when there are different agendas at work. We would state categorically that at the top of every issue is support of the museum—not the CEO, the staff, the trustees, the foundation, or individuals and donors. It is always, always, always about the museum. If the museum's trustees have done a good job in selecting the CEO, the museum has at its head an individual who knows what to do. Second-guessing him or making his job difficult is destructive. If the CEO is not competent, it is the responsibility of the museum trustees to remove him from that leadership position.

- The museum's trustees and the foundation members should meet together at least once a year to discuss issues of importance to the institution's future. If retreats are held to discuss the museum's strategic direction, foundation members should be included.

If you are a trustee at a museum that has more than one board, and if the problems discussed here sound even vaguely familiar, we urge you to work hard to remedy the situation, which hurts everyone but particularly hurts the museum. The problems are not difficult to fix; all that is required is the will to address them.

Not long ago we conducted a retreat that consisted of a museum's two boards, its CEO, and its staff. As we always do when planning a retreat, we asked the participants to tell us confidentially beforehand their two or three top issues and their hopes for the outcome of the retreat. Not surprisingly we heard a great deal about the problems of dealing with each other. The issue of working with two boards at odds with one another was obviously a major one for the museum. This issue was not on the surface; as is often the case, the comments made to us had never been discussed openly before. And so we dealt with them at the retreat.

At first the discussions were contentious. But before long each board, comprised of well-meaning people, began to *hear* what the members of the other board were saying. At the end of the day, the two board chairs made an executive decision, wholeheartedly supported by all members of both boards: From that day on, while keeping their separate identities for legal purposes, the two boards would meet and plan together. It was a fine moment, greeted with applause, and the museum will be much better served.

We believe that two boards, or possibly even three (a national, honorary board often makes up the third leg of the board stool), can offer the museum a great opportunity. There are more people with more contacts and more ideas to help the museum realize its goals. But again, as we have said before, it is the museum's goals and the museum's performance that are paramount.

Poor CEO

In chapter 3 we dealt in some detail with the identification, development, and evaluation of the CEO. Nevertheless, despite the best efforts, museums sometimes end up with weak CEOs or, worse, CEOs who are so incompetent, they can cause real damage.

This is one of those issues that can go unchecked for far too long. Perhaps it is because there is a certain delicacy about telling someone he is not doing a good job; perhaps it's too hard to deal with the emotion of such a meeting; or perhaps the board is tired and the idea of a search for a new CEO is unappealing at best. Still, it is the board's responsibility to deal with CEO problems quickly and fairly.

If the museum has limited resources, it may have recruited a CEO who is young or inexperienced or has never been in a leadership position before or maybe all three. If that is the case, it is the board's responsibility to understand the situation quickly, mentor the CEO and provide the necessary moral support, and take whatever steps are necessary to ensure that he has the necessary professional development opportunities to become a really good CEO.

A CEO who is new to the job may be a "slow starter," someone who is feeling his way through the intricacies of the museum, wanting to learn as much as he can before he begins to make decisions or comes to the board with serious issues. Again, the board must act quickly if the person seems less than satisfactory, and try to figure out the problem.

If the museum is really unlucky, the board just may have chosen the wrong person. Then it must fix the problem. It is the board's right to hire a CEO, and it is the board's responsibility to fire a CEO who is not performing adequately. If there are enough hard-minded business people on the board, this will be a non-issue and the problem will be taken care of. If the board has not yet recruited members from the business community, however, it may find the situation extremely uncomfortable. But it must be handled. That's why board members get the big bucks, right?

POOR RELATIONSHIP WITH THE CEO

From time to time a board of trustees will have a less than positive relationship with the museum's CEO. Sometimes the interactions are cool or distant, sometimes they are explosive and disruptive. But in every case, a poor relationship with the museum's CEO results in a dysfunctional situation and should be addressed.

There are a number of reasons why such a situation might arise, among them:
- CEO's resentment at poor board performance
- board's resentment at poor CEO performance
- CEO unable to keep up with the board's imagination
- board unable to keep up with the CEO's imagination
- lack of communication between the board and the CEO
- CEO uncomfortable with people of a different social class
- board uncomfortable with people of a different social class
- CEO suspicious of board
- board suspicious of CEO
- and the stuff of novels, someone with an agenda pitting board and CEO against one another

Any board member with a little experience could easily make up a list as quickly as we made up this one. But in our opinion the most important category falls in the middle of our list—lack of communication between the board and the CEO. Clear, open, and frequent communication between the CEO and the board is essential to a good relationship and good performance on the part of both. We do not mean to suggest that this is a simple problem; often it is distressingly complex. But we do want to encourage you to ensure that the lines of communication are wide open and flow in both directions.

If the issue is not a lack of communication or some variation of a misunderstanding, then the board must discover the cause and act to either repair or terminate the relationship. The board should not take action hastily, however. In our experience, situations such as this often result because of disappointed expectations, sometimes quite justified, on the part of the CEO, who may react in any number of ways, from subdued acquiescence to unreliable irritability, and often without ever clarifying the situation.

SUMMARY

Let's face it; life is full of troublesome people. Families have them, staff have them, and boards have them. The answer we all hope to find is the one that allows us to deal with these individuals with a minimum amount of damage to anyone. That isn't easy; it may not even be possible. And sometimes people who are perceived to be difficult really aren't; they simply may be the ones who provide the alternate point of view or question everything. The board needs such people, annoying as they sometimes are. We have noticed that if the board or CEO cannot answer their questions, these people are considered huge problems, and everyone wants to get rid of them. But if the answers are clear, the questioner is just considered a little annoying.

In a museum, there are procedures for handling difficult (in the true sense), divisive, or non-productive staff. Usually there is a probationary period at the beginning of employment, during which time the organization and the employee can assess whether the fit is right. At the end of the probationary period, the employee either is retained or told that he probably would be happier elsewhere. If truly disruptive people pass this screening, and they often do, or if the museum has a staff member who was hired before the probationary rule was established or has changed his at-work behavior, the museum can, and will, begin to document that individual. The process of documentation may take quite a while, but both the employee and employer are involved in the process. If the employee does not improve, and a good case has been made by the employer over a period of time, the employee can be legally terminated.

Most boards have a different problem; they often do not have a procedure or, sometimes, the will to deal with trustees who truly disrupt of their work. Earlier, we discussed some of the reasons for this reluctance to do the obvious, but the why of it does not really matter. Problem trustees can cause significant harm to the museum, and the board must face up to that fact and handle the problem in a straightforward way.

When it comes to dismissing someone, the board is not constrained the same way the museum is. Nevertheless firing a trustee should never be done in a capricious or hasty manner. The board chair, and probably the executive committee as well, must be assured that the trustee is a real problem and not the target of someone who wants to get him off the board. A variation of the institution's method for dealing with problem employees might work well. First, there must be a written procedure that lays out the process for dismissing a non-productive board member. The procedure should be discussed with trustees as part of the recruitment and orientation process, along with all the other things that are discussed at that time. Every new trustee should know that if his performance is not satisfactory, he will be asked to leave the board.

If a problem does arise, the board chair first should speak frankly to the trustee about the issue. At this time a probationary period should go into effect; for example, the trustee is told that he either changes his behavior during the next three months or he will be asked to leave the board. During the probationary period, the board chair should meet regularly with the trustee to chart his progress toward becoming a more productive member of the board.

There are two obvious problems with all of this:
- Board member terms may be so short that by the time the problem has been identified, talked through, and the probationary period finished, the person would have left the board anyway.
- Some behaviors are apparent only at board meetings, and many boards do not meet more than once every four months.

But it can be done; every museum will have to develop its own process depending upon the terms of trustees and the frequency of board meetings. And it must be done. The board has a basic responsibility to be the best that it can be and that does not mean only when it is convenient or unless you have to dismiss your best friend from the board. It is a simple statement: The board has a basic responsibility to be the best that it can be. If problems are not handled, there is a very good chance that the museum will suffer harm as a consequence.

Problem trustees must be dealt with fairly but quickly. There is no other option.

CHAPTER 7

When Boards Disappoint:
Fund Raising

CHAPTER 6 FOCUSES PRIMARILY ON SITUATIONS in which there is a problem with one or more trustees. But what should a CEO do when the problem is with the board as a whole? More to the point, how can the board recognize that there is a problem and work to address it?

We have decided to focus on only one issue in this section—the board that does not, cannot, or will not fund raise. This problem appears to be as ubiquitous as salt in the ocean; directors talk about it, staff talk about it, consultants talk about it, and sometimes boards talk about it. And still it is a problem; perhaps because while all these groups are talking, they are not talking to each other.

If the topic is fund raising, we would say no one can do it better than the board, but often, no one tries to avoid it more than the board. Why? There are no clear answers, although the results are obvious. When a museum board neglects its fund-raising role, the institution suffers greatly. Without the resources it needs to fulfill its mission, its programs languish and grow stale; it cannot grow and try new things; morale suffers; visibility diminishes; essential building maintenance is deferred; and the museum is unable to serve either its internal or its external communities very well. In addition, the staff usually resents the fact that the board is not providing the support that they understand as one of the board's fundamental responsibilities, and there is a split, usually an unacknowledged split, between board and staff. Sometimes the board is aware of this; sometimes it is not. But in either case, the stage set for future failure slowly is being furnished.

In a for-profit enterprise, a red flag goes up the instant the revenue line goes flat, and fireworks explode if it goes down. The source of the problem is identified, and the CEO and/or non-functioning board members are disciplined and probably forced out of the organization—i.e., "heads will roll." In a museum with a volunteer board, a less corporate and more collegial atmosphere generally exists, and unclear expectations and a fuzzy definition of responsibilities often cloud the picture. Since some variation of a gentleman's agreement pervades relationships between the CEO and his board of trustees, deference and polite acceptance on the CEO's part may obscure the true nature of the problem. Sometimes concerns are not even addressed, delicacy prohibiting such "accusatory" behavior, and the board continues to operate in the dark.

While the CEO is clearly at fault in such a situation, the board also bears part of the blame. Boards are composed of intelligent and well-connected people, who are used to thinking about and working with money. Why should they have to be told that they need to raise money? Fund raising is one of an organization's most quantifiable activities. An F on the fund-raising report card is an F no matter how the figures are manipulated, and anyone should be able to see it. And yet responsibility for fund raising often slides off the shoulders of the board and onto the CEO, or the staff, or even the economy. In our experience, nowhere is the relationship between CEO and board so frequently tested as in an organization where the board's fund-raising role is not clearly understood.

When asked about this, board members have several general responses at the ready:
- Fund raising is the job of the CEO and museum staff.
- Board members do not know how to fund raise.
- Board members are uncomfortable with the idea of fund raising.
- No one ever said board members would have to fund raise.

Three key points are missing from these responses: 1) Fund raising is one of the board's fundamental responsibilities. 2) No one is better positioned to raise money than the trustees. 3) There is no museum in this country, in the world, that could not use more money.

Let's look at each of these points in turn.

Fund Raising Is a Fundamental Responsibility of the Board of Trustees

In chapter 2 we discussed the fundamental duties of individual trustees and the board as a whole. We suggested that, in addition to being responsible for their own performance, trustees have four major roles to play: loyalty to the museum's mission; care of the museum's assets; service to the community;

and responsibility for the board's performance. Even if fund raising had not been specifically mentioned, and it was, common sense would tell you that the board must raise money to enable fulfillment of the mission; ensure care for the assets, both human and artifact; and enhance service to the community. Museum trusteeship is neither a passive occupation nor a military one; it is a relationship of trust, partnership, and support, the beneficiary being the museum itself.

No One Is Better Positioned to Raise Money than the Trustees

As we have said before, we cannot overestimate the importance of building a good and strong board, composed of trustees that fully understand their responsibilities to the museum and the special qualities they bring to the museum's work. It is without a doubt one of the key elements in the museum's ability to fulfill its promise to educate, inspire, and provide value to the community. Carefully selected, board members can position the museum locally, and often nationally, far more effectively than anyone else. They are, if they were chosen strategically (see chapter 4), the museum's primary link to the community. Their ability to connect to influential people in both the public and private sectors and to raise funds to support the museum is unquestioned. Furthermore, their visibility and prestige make them extremely valuable advocates for the museum.

There Is No Museum in this Country, in the World, that Could Not Use More Money

Museum-going is a heavily subsidized activity, and the money must come from somewhere. The museum's funds can never keep pace with its ambition, creativity, imagination, drive, and desire to take the world by storm; shake off the "dusty and dull" image the word "museum" carries for so many people; and streak across the historical and cultural landscape, brightening people's lives in significant ways.

Unless the museum's staff and board raise money, the museum will not be able to grow and change, care for its collections, realize its future vision, or serve its audiences well. It will not be able to maintain its physical plant or pay competitive wages to its staff; it will not be able to market itself and its programs; it will not be able to provide outreach, in-reach, or Web-site access. It will not be able to change people's lives.

Clearly no one is likely to argue that fund raising is the trustees' sole responsibility because the important strategic work of museum boards is well understood. But the fund-raising conversation is one that many museum administrators would like to have with their boards. All the fine feeling associated with the board's involvement in the museum—attending programs and meetings, working in partnership with the CEO, providing direction, and ensuring that the museum's finances are carefully and accurately kept—evaporates when the museum needs to raise private money for its operations or a capital project, and the board either cannot or will not play a major role in the fund-raising effort.

Boards have been in existence for a long time, and so has this problem. Why, then, is nothing done about it? Why do so many new trustees know so much about the museum's programs but so little about the board's role in funding those programs?

We have observed five common conditions that may answer this question:

1. The board may not have formal expectations for its members.
2. The board may have an "expectations" document but it does not discuss fund raising.
3. The board has fund-raising criteria, but the recruiter either doesn't agree with them or knows that the board doesn't follow them.
4. The recruiter doesn't want to insult an influential member of the community by suggesting that the museum wants more than his intelligence and reasoning ability at the board meetings.
5. The recruiter doesn't want to lose a good candidate

The first point is the most important: Many people join boards of trustees without understanding the fundamental expectations for service. It is the main reason boards do not function as fund raisers in the way that they could and should. Boards in this situation miss the opportunity to bring together a group of people, united by purpose and mission, who can focus on the museum's vision for the future and ensure that it becomes a reality.

Point 2 reflects a board that either is not aware of its responsibility in the area of fund raising or is unwilling to accept it. Points 3, 4, and 5 reflect how individual trustees may feel about the board's criteria, if they have them, or that they don't want the criteria to get in the way of recruitment. But why recruit someone who does not know what his responsibilities are, and may be unwilling to perform them when he does find out? What a waste of a board seat. If the last three points describe your board, it means that the board is not asserting its authority over individual members. If points 1 or 2 sound familiar, a vote and revision of the expectations document can help remedy the situation. The next step, of course, will be to communicate openly with new board recruits.

Unless they are told otherwise, potential trustees might assume that the staff takes care of fund raising, the endowment adequately supplements earned revenue, or admissions revenue is sufficient to support the museum. They may not fully understand how very different the museum is from the businesses they are associated with, that the sale of the museum's product (the exhibitions, activities, and programs that bring in admissions revenue) covers perhaps one-third of the costs to produce that product, and that the museum depends in large part on contributed revenue for its survival.

It is important to clear this up so that you and the potential trustee will know if the fit is right. And then, you will need to know:

- whether the recruit already has fund-raising obligations for another organization
- whether the recruit is uncomfortable with, or opposed to, serving as a door opener and fund raiser for the museum

A recruiter for the board might tell a potential candidate something like this:

> One of our basic responsibilities is to the museum's financial sustainability. In the same way that a business must sell a product, this institution must sell its mission. And it stays in business and supports its programs by raising money from people who see the value that it adds to the community. Fund raising is a basic responsibility of all board members, and all are expected to participate in some way. In addition, each board member is expected to make a personal annual contribution to the museum; this is important in terms of our own personal credibility when seeking funds from others.

This is a message that is impossible to misunderstand and allows a potential recruit to respond, either positively or negatively, at the beginning, when it really counts. The white gloves are off, and the professional mantle is on. As it should be.

We have discussed some general reasons that board members give for their reluctance to participate in fund raising. But there are some specific reasons, too, some quite legitimate:

- Many board members object to their fund-raising role because they see it as manipulating their friends and business associates.
- There can be, and often are, strings attached to a charitable contribution made by one friend to another, a *quid pro quo*, sometimes dollar for dollar— i.e., my charity for your charity.
- Often board members don't want to participate in fund raising because they just don't know how.

A board can go a long way toward overcoming its reluctance to fund raise with a little training from a professional fund-raising consultant. Fund-raising workshops can be a lot of fun, and often represent the first time that trustees have heard "money" talked about so openly. Generally the workshops begin with an introduction to fund raising, where participants learn the jargon of the trade—prospect research, prospects, cultivation, the ask, lapsed donors (whom development directors sometimes refer to as "Lybunt," meaning that they gave "last year but unfortunately not this"), naming opportunity, the gift. Trustees are told why people give or don't give, how to match a donor's interests with the needs of the museum, and what to do when you are told no. And there are always wonderful stories of the things people have been able to accomplish by giving their money away. The tone and the message for this part of the workshop are likely to fall somewhere between religious experience and pep talk.

Once the stage for fund raising has been set and the museum's priorities have been examined, the consultant will take trustees through an "ask," step by step. Then it is the trustees' turn. This part of the workshop is usually very entertaining, as trustees pull out all the stops to ask each other for large sums of money or participate by role-playing a very tough "ask." If the workshop is done well, by the end participants will be laughing and having a good time, and a good part of their fear will have been replaced by confidence and excitement. If nothing else, all the talk about money—who has it, who doesn't have it, who wants it, who gets it—helps trustees to overcome their usual sensitivity about the subject, at least in the context of the museum.

As trustees become more practiced fund raisers, they will begin to understand that in some very real ways they are providing a service to the donor as well as to the museum. In other words, they are not sneaking up on a reluctant wallet. The museum, with its important mission and ambitious vision for the future, needs money to realize its goals, and many donors want, or need, to give away money. Trustees should remember that the museum provides satisfaction not only to themselves but to others as well. If the money doesn't come to their museum, it's going to go somewhere else, and that would be a shame.

Money is an enabler. In the case of the Great Museum, it can enable more and better programs; a deeper connection with the community; a closer relationship with schools, families, scholars, and researchers; and an opportunity to make a difference to the way people see the world. It can provide a way for a donor to make an important contribution to the life of the community, a contribution that can have an impact for years into the future. A donor who is never asked cannot give, and research has shown that there are an extraordinary number of people who are never asked and who would gladly give if they were asked.

In the interim, before they attend those fund-raising workshops and just for practice, trustees should think about a potential museum donor, the members of the board, and the museum's priorities together as a package, as follows:

- What might the donor want? (This is usually not articulated and sometimes not even consciously known.) For example, is it visibility within the community, the education of children, life-long learning, institutional capacity building, technology, specific exhibition topics, programs, accessibility for people with disabilities, a tax write-off for a good cause?
- Does the donor want to honor someone in a very special way?
- What else could the museum offer, consistent with its mission and priorities, that would be an appropriate vehicle of support for this donor?
- Who knows this donor or has the closest connection to him?

The bottom line is that museum fund raising is about matching a person's interests with the needs of the museum. The role of the board is to find, in the most positive sense, a good fit between the museum and the interests of their friends, family, acquaintances, contacts, and prospects identified by others.

Board members should remember that the reason someone might contribute to the museum is probably similar to the reason the board member agreed to serve in the first place. It's about:

- what the museum does
- the outcome of what it does
- its value to the world beyond its walls
- the constituency it serves
- its unique ability to deliver on its promises
- the difference it can make in people's lives through education and inspiration

This entire discussion assumes that board members believe in the importance of the work of the museum and are truly excited about the value it adds to the community. Fund raising is nothing more than explaining, with enthusiasm, what drew you to the museum in the first place and how your life has been enhanced as a result. It is about explaining the satisfaction you feel at seeing how each contribution of time and money helps the museum to do its job. And it is about playing a role in the museum's work.

When a board, individually and collectively, understands and accepts its role as fund raiser, and the staff has a powerful partner in this difficult task, it is important that all carry the same clear message to the museum's friends and potential donors, and everyone else for that matter.

One document, called the case statement, should lay out the key points to be made. A well-thought-out and articulated case statement ensures that board and staff agree about the direction of the museum and its fundamental messages and that all tell the same story when they go out on the institution's behalf. The board must be involved in the development of the case statement, which should explain the museum's mission, short- and long-term goals, and the value it adds to the community. Whatever form the case statement takes, it must raise excitement about the museum's vision and its specific contributions to the community.

To give you something to think about, we suggest that a case statement answer the following questions:
- Why is the museum important?
- What value does it add to the community?
- What are its core messages?
- What community needs does it address?
- What makes the museum distinctive?
- Who is the audience for its exhibitions and programs?

- What would be lost if the museum didn't exist?
- What are the museum's goals for the future?
- What are the museum's priorities for this campaign, and why?
- What, specifically, are you requesting from this donor?

A case statement provides a solid foundation on which even the most reluctant board fund raiser can stand with confidence, any time, any place, in front of anyone.

Before we leave this topic, let's clarify the fund-raising roles of the board and staff, keeping in mind that there are no hard and fast rules that apply to everyone. There are, however, some base-line fundamentals that you might consider. Sorted in their broadest terms, the roles are as follows:

The Board
- The board members help the staff develop a list of potential supporters.
- The board members use their contacts in the community to increase the museum's visibility.
- The board members open doors for the museum's CEO and staff.
- The board members respond to requests from staff for assistance with particular donors, whether individuals, corporations, or foundations.
- The board members participate in or host cultivation events.
- The board members ask for significant contributions from their peers and prospects identified by the museum.
- The board members lobby legislators for support for the museum.
- The board members use their names to ensure success of museum special events.
- The board members host donor cultivation or recognition events at their homes, when appropriate.
- The board members make annual gifts to the museum, appropriate to their ability.

The Staff
- The staff provides administrative support to the board.
- The staff provides prospect research where appropriate.
- The staff plans and executes events that recognize donors.
- The staff asks for the board to help with particular donors.

- The staff responds to requests from board members for assistance with particular donors.
- The staff accompanies the board on fund-raising calls, when appropriate.
- The staff ensures that an annual fund for unrestricted gifts is in place.
- The staff ensures that the museum has fund-raising activity in the following additional areas: corporations, foundations, individual donors, planned gifts, estate gifts.
- The staff keeps track of all donor records and makes sure that donors are contacted on a regular basis, either via museum promotional materials or a special call, depending upon the nature of the gift.
- The staff makes annual gifts to the museum, appropriate to their ability.

SUMMARY

The issue that we have described in this chapter is a serious one for museums and their boards of trustees. Private fund raising is central to the museum's ability to perform; consequently, it is an important board responsibility. And yet, as we mentioned earlier, this is the area in which boards most often fail. Since it is obvious that no board would turn its back on one of its major obligations, we believe that there is a great deal of misunderstanding around this topic; and the symptoms can be found in museums large and small in every part of the country. We chose to give this topic its own chapter because we believe it is important to call attention to it. Now it is up to you—those of you who see your boards described in this chapter—to do something about it. As we have mentioned throughout this book, change must come from within the board. The call for change may come from outside—from the CEO, a consultant, this book—but if no one on the board is listening or even wants to listen, nothing will change.

In a museum, there will always be issues that keep boards and staffs from doing their best. Since all parties are genuinely committed to the museum and want to leave a lasting positive legacy, there is seldom anyone to blame for the problems or misunderstandings that arise. The only rational thing to do is to fix whatever is broken. In the case of fund raising, this will mean more tightly defining the board's criteria for new member recruitment, sticking to those criteria, and implementing the processes and training that will ensure that board members are comfortable and successful fund raisers on the museum's behalf.

In some ways boards are at a disadvantage because of the very power that they hold. Often no one is willing to risk enough to question the quality of the board's performance, and board members are not told directly that there are problems or what the problems are. They operate under the impression that all is going well and that they are universally loved, when, in fact, they are being privately disparaged by the staff and others. We see this happen most often around the issue of board fund raising, and we take offense on behalf of boards, believing that it is unfair to expect trustees to change when they don't know that anyone thinks they should change. Most boards are quite pleased with their own performance and, if no one says differently, why shouldn't they be?

But once told, a board must deal with the issue, whatever it is, in a straight-forward manner. Let the messenger live; in fact, reward the messenger for doing something that's very hard to do—face a strong and powerful board of trustees with bad news, or worse, pointed criticism. In no other way will the board be able to contribute all that it can to ensure the museum's success.

CHAPTER 8

Summary and Conclusions

An accreditable museum has a clear sense of mission and organizes its governing authority, staff, financial resources, collections, public programs, and activities to meet its formally stated mission. —AAM

SEVERAL YEARS AGO, WE WORKED with a museum that was fortunate enough to have a high-powered board. The individual trustees were well connected in the community, able to bring considerable personal resources to the museum and provide significant support in fund raising, enthusiastically committed to the museum's success, and had a good working partnership with the CEO. Thus, when the museum CEO asked us to "help [her] board members understand what 'good' means in a museum," we were puzzled.

As we worked with the CEO and the board we began to understand a bit more about the dilemma. The museum's board was made up of trustees from corporations, small businesses, and the professions and also included philanthropists and several subject-matter scholars. They were extremely intelligent and committed individuals and very involved in the life of the museum. But they held very traditional views of what a museum should be and how it should operate. The CEO had been pressuring for change and the board had been surprisingly resistant; finally she realized that, in some ways, she had been speaking to them in a foreign language. Despite the fact that they were completely engaged in their work, their vision of a museum had been formed when they were much younger. The stately, the old, the valuable, the intrinsic good of the artifact, the quiet, the dignified, the respectable and respectful, the prestige of a good museum—these were all part of their frame of reference.

While she respected the traditions of the past and the venerable old building the museum inhabited, the CEO was looking to the future and finding that the road the institution needed to take was not the road it was on. Competition for people's leisure time had increased, and museum-goers' expectations had changed. Visitors now expected to be engaged, involved, and drawn in to the museum's exhibitions; they were no longer willing to play the role of empty vessels, waiting for someone to pour in the knowledge. People began to question the museum's story as well as the old-fashioned display and exhibition techniques it used. And new audiences—nosier, suspicious, challenging—were demanding to be included.

The situation was particularly uncomfortable because of the high quality of the board members themselves. There was a core group of strong trustees who considered themselves museum experts, after accepting, and carrying out admirably, service on a museum board and learning a great deal in the process. But most of these trustees had not been in a museum for a very long time; the demands of their lives meant they didn't have the time to visit any museums on a regular basis, let alone those experimenting with different ways of reaching audiences and embracing an entirely different standard for "good." While they liked and respected the CEO, they were not ready for the kind of macro-change she was proposing.

We decided not to show the trustees what "good" looked like; after all, one person's "good" is another's "travesty." Instead, we focused on the museum's mission, vision for the future, and strategic plan. We recommended a planning retreat that would involve both board and senior staff, asserting from the beginning that everything was open for discussion. As we always do before a retreat, we asked each board and staff member to tell us the two or three issues regarding the museum's future that concerned them most. We promised to keep these concerns confidential, although we promised to bring them up ourselves, unattributed, if the discussions would benefit as a result.

As we read through the confidential communications that were sent to us, we discovered several interesting things about the board:

- Not everyone on the board agreed about the current mission and direction.
- A small group of board members tended to dominate discussions and assert expertise that others did not challenge.
- No one on the board could validate the CEO's position from his own experience or point of view.
- While many board members did not understand the CEO's concern, they were willing to learn.

Fortunately this was an easy problem to solve. The planning retreat was exciting and stimulating. The discussion of the mission revealed right away that it no longer suited the museum's circumstances, and the group began to work on a new statement. But the tide really turned when we asked board and staff to talk about their vision for the museum's future. Once this group of intelligent, motivated individuals began to engage this question, it became obvious that change was needed to achieve their dreams. The CEO proposed that the board visit museums in other parts of the country that were experimenting with interactive and engaging exhibitions that had high-entertainment as well as high-educational value. The board endorsed the idea enthusiastically.

For us, the process reinforced several of the points we have made in this book. Taking this situation as an example, you can readily see that:

- The board did not have a climate of open discussion during its meetings, no matter how collegial it seemed.
- The board had not disciplined its members.
- The board was missing critical expertise among its members.
- The board was not as close to its community as it should have been.
- The board did not understand how changes in the museum field and in museum audiences affected its own institution.
- The CEO-board partnership was only strong if the CEO did not seriously challenge the board (or rather, as it turned out, certain board members).
- The board had neglected the issue of mission, vision, and direction for too long.

Many museum boards would avoid most of the problems that keep them from being exemplary if they would ensure that the museum has a thoughtfully developed mission, vision, and strategic plan; that the board participates fully in the development of these three essential building blocks; and that the museum uses these guiding documents as a measure for all plans, programs, activities, and opportunities. The mission is the gyroscope that will keep the museum balanced; the vision will ensure that it is looking into the future, and the plan will organize the work of both board and staff so they can achieve the museum's ambition.

For the board to be strong and effective, the board members and the CEO must trust each other enough to engage in serious debate about issues important to the museum. A climate of openness with a minimum of defensiveness and a maximum of inquiry will go a long way toward ensuring the strength of your board and the museum.

If we are concerned for renewal, we will encourage a measure of diversity and dissent. Dissent is not comfortable, but generally it is simply the proposing of alternatives—and a system that is not continuously examining alternatives is not likely to evolve creatively."—John W. Gardner, *National Renewal*, September 1995. Published by Independent Sector and the National Civic League.

In this book, we have talked quite a bit about how to have a strong board. We will not revisit that topic in detail here, except to remind you that a strong board *begins* with an understanding of the museum's mission and a strong partnership with the museum's CEO, and then with recruitment of board members, chosen from defined criteria, who will be able to help the museum achieve its mission. Chapters 4 and 5 dealt with this issue specifically, although, really, it is what the whole book is about. We believe that good board work is critical to the achievement of the museum's vision. It ensures that the museum has strong leadership, the resources to do its work in the world, an appropriate mission and vision, and plans that will allow it to achieve those high ideals. It ensures that the museum's assets, both its collections and its staff, are cared for, and that once direction is set for the museum, it stays the course. It ensures that trustees understand their role and are willing to analyze both their own and the entire board's performance and make course corrections where necessary.

One way to begin a discussion among the trustees about the board's real contribution to the museum would be to devote several hours at your next meeting to a discussion of the following topics:

- What does our board contribute that the museum would not have without us?

- How has the board developed in the last four years, and is it for the better? If the answer to this question is no, how can the board improve?

- How has the museum developed in the last four years, and is it for the better? Whether the answer is yes or no, what has been the board's role in the change?

- What would the CEO say about us if we were not in the room?

- What would the staff say about us if we were not in the room?

- What would the museum's constituents say about us if we were not in the room?

The board evaluation process that we discussed in chapter 5 includes input from people outside the board and even outside the museum, when appropriate. But for a beginning discussion, a mini-self-analysis, use the questions above, and make sure that your conversation is open, honest, and brave.

We also suggest that the board craft a mission for its own work, if it doesn't already have one. As we discussed in chapter 5, a board's mission can be simple and straightforward, focused on helping the museum fulfill its mission and make a difference in the life of its community. Notice that while we recognize the authority of the board as the museum's governing body, throughout this book we have stressed the board's *service* to the museum. This is its true role, and it is defined in several ways:

- responsibility to ensure the best possible professional leadership for the museum and support the staff and CEO in the discharge of their duties
- responsibility to ensure sufficient funds to support the mission and achieve the vision and plan of the museum
- responsibility to provide connections to the community
- responsibility to ensure care of the collections, physical plant, and employees
- responsibility to ensure consistency of focus and direction as described in the museum's mission
- responsibility to understand the museum's programs and services and provide advice based on community knowledge

This articulation of the board's role is significantly different from the "oversight" role assumed by many boards. We do not diminish the board's responsibilities to ensure that the museum is in compliance with legal and ethical standards. We simply extend that role, and shift the board's thinking in a practical sense away from oversight and toward partnership and service. When the system is working well, everyone serves the museum; staff and board have one guiding star, the mission, and all work together to achieve it. Behind this is the assumption that boards take very seriously their mandate to hire competent professional management, i.e., the CEO, and provide that person with the necessary support and mentoring. That makes the functional oversight role, while important, far less critical, and service to the mutually held mission and vision far more important, to the museum's future success.

Almost every museum has a board, but not every museum has a good board. We believe that this is a huge waste of talent; our experience has introduced us to a wide variety of trustees, extraordinary individuals, willing to give their time and resources to enhance the quality of a museum and ensure a significant community asset. This is real public service, and we are all the better for it.

But all too frequently, when a group of talented individuals come together, they seem to create something that is less than the sum of their individual parts. One way to achieve board success is to consider that it may be the result of partnership opportunities, embraced openly and trustingly on many levels:

- There is the partnership between individual board members that encourages an atmosphere of trust and professionalism, enabling the most difficult discussions to be held in a non-personal manner.
- There is the partnership between the board and the CEO, who must communicate openly and honestly with each other and never allow the other to be surprised by an issue of significance.
- There is the partnership between the board and the staff, which allows the board to support and mentor staff where appropriate, but insists that board members step back from interference in the work of the staff.
- There is the partnership between the board and the museum's donors, ensuring that the donors' money is well spent, that contributions go to their designated projects, and that donors are appropriately thanked and honored.
- There is the partnership between the board and the museum's audiences, and the charge to the board to stay close to these audiences, learning what they like and don't like about the museum and working to make the experience a better one for anyone who steps through the doors.
- There is the partnership between the board and the community, where the board protects and serves a significant community asset, making the community itself a better place in which to live, work, and visit.

When any of these partnerships is neglected, the board does itself and the museum a disservice.

We seem to have developed a fondness for lists during the course of writing this book, and so we will leave you with just one more—some suggestions about how the board should work with two of its most important partners, the museum's staff and CEO:

- agree on mission, vision, and goals
- agree on institutional priorities
- agree on a timetable for the goals and priorities
- assign responsibility and ensure accountability for the museum's priorities
- identify and know the organization's key stakeholders
- identify and recruit the best possible board members
- agree on role of board
- agree on role of the CEO and staff
- ensure annual review of the museum's strategic plan
- ensure annual review of the CEO
- ensure annual review of board performance
- agree on clear measures of success

We believe that if all museum boards systematically work their way through this list, they will go a good way toward being the best they can be, i.e., the Ideal Board.

But the final caveat we leave you with is this: Unless a board is willing to admit to internal problems (if it has them) or, as we have stressed over and over, willing to enforce its own authority over individual trustees, it will be less than it can be. Whether the issue is a problem trustee, conflict of interest, ineffective board chair, micromanagement of staff, or the board's culture, the board must 1) acknowledge that there is a problem; 2) recognize that it is the board's responsibility to fix the problem; and 3) fix the problem. When a board is united on the first two points, there will be plenty of help for the third.

Good luck. Your work is tremendously important, and you affect the success of all of the country's museums and, by extension, the cultural life and education of all of its citizens. We salute you, we thank you for all that you do, and we wish you well.

CHAPTER 9

Cases for Reading and Discussion

THIS CHAPTER INCLUDES A SERIES OF CASES, studies of various fictional institutions that are addressing (or not addressing) problem situations. While these cases are not based on real-life incidents, the situations are fairly common and hence quite "real" in the world of museums. There is no one right answer to any of these problems; in fact, there are different ways of looking at, and several legitimate solutions for, each of them. Since the cases are fictional and in no way connected to your own institution, you can examine the situations and people with complete objectivity, exploring potential action steps without fear of offending anyone.

Working with these cases will give you an opportunity to practice group discussions about serious and important issues without the baggage that typically hinders straight talk in real-life situations, with personal relationships at the top of the list. Sooner or later something will have the potential to disrupt the equilibrium of your board or even your museum. Our experience has been that discussion of difficult or controversial issues degenerates far too quickly from the professional level it should occupy into a personal slug fest that can have no good outcome. The real issue often gets lost in a thicket of personal sensitivities, unquestioned assumptions, and the presumed entitlements of social position or assertions of expertise. If you have not learned to discuss volatile situations dispassionately and professionally, when an issue does arise that affects *your museum*, the board certainly—and the museum probably—will be at risk.

The cases we have selected are also stories. We wrote them this way because stories can sometimes show what we can't see otherwise. We do not claim literary expertise; rather, we seek to provide fictional distance from the situations and characters, thus allowing you to see the various points of view more clearly than if you were directly involved. You may even recognize something that is at work in your own museum, something that you may not have noticed before. Through the use of these story-cases, we hope to give you new eyes and provide the opportunity for some stimulating discussions.

The stories that we have chosen to include in this book are:

- "Slow Drift": The board of the Franklin J. Miller Museum of History thinks its CEO is unproductive. But is he?
- "The Crowell Pinter Exhibition": The museum's board has agreed to exhibit the collection of one of its own trustees, and an unfriendly reporter causes trouble.
- "A Capital Experience": The director of the Foley Museum considers canceling a new capital campaign, even though the museum desperately needs the money.
- "Whose Museum?" This vignette is about the effect a very strong personality, in this case the museum's founder, has on the board.
- "Does One Plus One = Two, or Trouble?" This lucky museum is operating with two boards, and it's getting harder and harder.
- "The Surprise": The Stone Town Museum's board chair bypasses the director to get funding for a pet project of her own.
- "Does Better Mean Bigger?" The board has approved purchase of a $5-million building adjacent to the building now occupied by the historical society; is the organization ready for this type of expansion?
- "The Dinner Party": A new board chair discovers what some local residents really think about the museum.

Several of these cases have been written from the CEO's point of view because it is easier to get at some issues through the CEO's eyes than through the eyes of the board. Our purpose in these vignettes is to show the viewpoint of a major museum stakeholder who appears powerless to alter what seems to be a disastrous course. This also may help show why we insist that board issues are museum concerns. How the board functions is extremely important to the success of the museum and affects the CEO's ability to work with the board to the museum's best advantage.

We hope that you will enjoy these story-cases and that they will give you interesting topics to think and talk about. As we have said before, there is no right answer to any of them, and there are many answers to all of them. A good way to get a broad range of solutions and opinions is to set aside a couple of hours; divide the board into small groups, each tackling the same case; deliberate for 20 minutes or so; and report back to the larger group. Such discussions will help train trustees for the open and direct conversations that are essential to good board work and the development of a depersonalized atmosphere for discussion. It will be interesting to see if you all handle the various issues in the same way, or if there are differences in approach and, perhaps, in opinion.

For each case there are two main issues to be considered:
  1) how the situation might have been avoided
  2) what to do now

We have included other questions at the end of each case, but these two are basic to every situation. We encourage you to engage in debate and disagree with and challenge each other as you work through these cases. These exercises are designed to prepare you for a future in which, sooner or later, there will be a real problem that will require careful, thoughtful, and de-personalized deliberation. Please remember the two words that characterize good board discussions: honesty and courage.

SLOW DRIFT

The board of the Franklin J. Miller Museum of History couldn't decide what to do about the museum's new director, Dr. David Cuttle. No one thought David was doing a particularly good job, but a number of board members did not want to go through another search process. It was expensive, they argued, and obviously not particularly effective. Besides, David had been at the museum for less than a year; maybe he needed to get used to the place before he decided what he wanted to do. In any case, no one could point to a specific problem; it was just that nothing much seemed to be happening. The former director, Joe Sontag, always had something going on—plans for new exhibitions, plans for fund raising, plans to involve schoolchildren. Board Chair Martin Goldman and many of the trustees thought that David was allowing the museum to coast on its past successes, and they were impatient. While they realized that it would take a while for someone to take hold of a job as complex as the directorship of the Miller Museum, they felt that by now more should be happening. It seemed to them that David Cuttle had no vision for the organization.

As the monthly board meeting broke up, Goldman watched everyone walk out of the room. Once more David Cuttle had presented no plans to the board. It was as if the museum was adrift.

The last trustee to leave, Cissy McDonald, stopped at the door and looked back at him. He looked tired and worried. She turned and came toward him, still buttoning her coat for the winter blowing outside. "What do you think, Martin? What should we do?"

There was no need to ask what she meant; they had talked about the Cuttle problem many times over the last several months.

Martin looked up and sighed. "I don't know, Cissy. No one wants to go through another search. It's exhausting. Besides, we haven't ever formally discussed David's performance, much less firing him."

Cissy tugged a brown knit hat over her short bobbed hair. "It's pretty hard to talk about him when he's right here with us all the time."

Martin nodded. "All the conversations about him have taken place away from the meeting—and in phone calls I'm getting. You're probably getting them, too."

"Yes, the board is restless," said Cissy, pulling on her gloves, "but I'm not sure we have completely defined the problem. We just talk about being dissatisfied—maybe it's just a personality thing. He isn't very charismatic."

"To say the least. But no, I think it's more than that. We are expecting strong direction for the museum, leadership, and we aren't getting it."

Cissy nodded. "Have you talked to him about it?"

"Of course. Several times. He doesn't seem to understand what I'm saying."

"Does he have any response? Any plans? I could understand if he wasn't ready to present anything to the board yet, but surely he would confide in you."

Martin rested his elbows on the conference table. "That's just it. He seems to think he has a lot going on."

Cissy's eyes widened. "How could he think that? He isn't doing anything."

Martin sighed. "He points to the "Influence of Africa" exhibit, and the Children's Room as new initiatives."

Cissy snorted. "Those were both planned before Joe left; you know that. You have to take control, Martin."

He shrugged and stood up slowly. Gathering his papers together, he said, "First I have to get a better handle on what's really going on. His qualifications for this job were good. It doesn't make sense to think that he can't do it. It's quite possible that a lot is going on, and we just don't know about it."

"Even if that's true, that's not so good, is it? The museum's plans and projects shouldn't come to the board like birthday presents, all pre-selected and wrapped."

"No, but that would be better than nothing, which is what I'm afraid is happening. I wonder what the staff is thinking."

"How can you find out?"

"I think I'll talk to Ed Lance. He has been at the museum longer than anyone;

in fact, I've been encouraging David to make him his deputy. And he's very well respected inside the museum. Now there's a man who could lead this place."

"He would have been perfect," Cissy agreed.

Martin nodded. "Yes, he wanted the job, I'm pretty sure of it, but at the time there was a strong push from some members of the board to bring in someone from outside, someone with a fresh viewpoint and more experience. I didn't push it, and Ed didn't push it."

"Can he be objective?" asked Cissy. "If he wanted this job himself?"

Martin shrugged. "I think so. I'll talk to him quietly, away from the museum. Somehow I need to know more than I do right now about this situation."

MARTIN CALLED ED AS SOON AS HE REACHED HIS OFFICE: "I need to see you," he said. "Soon." He glanced down at the telephone messages that had accumulated during his absence.

"Sure, Martin. What's it about?" Ed's no-nonsense Midwestern twang was comforting.

"I'd rather not say until we get together." Martin looked at his calendar. "How about tomorrow, here at my office, say 7:00 a.m.?"

"O.K.," said Ed, clearly puzzled. "I'll be there."

WHEN ED WALKED INTO THE OFFICES of Goldman-Weintraub exactly at 7:00 a.m., Martin was already there, working at his desk. He had obviously been there for some time, judging from the papers spread in piles across his desk. He looked up sheepishly. "I get my best work done early in the morning. Drives my wife crazy."

Ed smiled. "Ellen's the early riser in our house. I'd probably sympathize with your wife."

Martin chuckled. "Most people do," he said. Then he became more serious as he invited Ed to sit in the large leather chair on the other side of the desk. "I asked you to meet me, Ed, because I wanted to discuss a problem we're having at the museum." He hesitated and then went on. "Frankly, it's about David's leadership?"

Ed looked surprised as he shifted his position slightly. "What do you mean?"

Martin's look was direct and probing. He hesitated for a moment and then said, "I mean, do you think he's doing a good job?"

Ed looked away. He could feel the heat rising in his face. This was an extremely uncomfortable situation. David was a nice man, but he just hadn't taken hold of the museum. Ed could understand why the board was concerned. Not that anyone had moved to help the new director. The staff had all been there for a long time, and David was an outsider. Ed could probably have helped but he was busy with his own work. Besides, he didn't have that kind of relationship with David, and David hadn't asked.

It was legitimate for the board to think that David hadn't put his own stamp on the place, but the new director didn't have much room to maneuver. Joe Sontag had been director for more than 20 years, but had done less and less as he grew closer to retirement. The staff, intensely loyal to Joe, had planned a lot of things on their own, just to keep the museum's level of activity high. And Joe had allowed it because he knew the staff was competent and because it made him look good. For example, "Influence of Africa" and the Children's Room were moving forward at a rapid pace, even though neither David nor Joe had much to do with either of them. The upside was that there was activity; the downside was that the museum's human and financial resources were stretched as the institution developed according to the staff's personal interests.

The staff's fondness for and loyalty to Joe had not yet transferred to David. In fact, they were highly suspicious of the new director. They liked the way things had been done in the past, and now they were feeling over-extended, even though they had over-extended themselves. Ed wasn't sure but he suspected that several staff members were making life difficult for David on purpose. They didn't produce anything he asked for—even simple background information—until he had asked for it two or three times. It would be hard for anyone to do much under these circumstances. David would have to deal with the staff before he could make much progress on anything, and apparently he hadn't mentioned any of this to the board. Ed felt a twinge of guilt for not having helped David more, and he could have. Instead he had just retreated into his own work. Why?

A storm was building up outside and Ed was momentarily distracted by the sound of the wind rattling the windows. Martin's office was on the 25th floor of the Banneker Building, and Ed was certain the windows shouldn't be rattling like that. He forced himself to look back at Martin and back into consideration of this uncomfortable situation. Ed knew he would have moved faster to correct the situation if he had been director, not that the staff would have stone-walled him. David certainly had his problems—Ed glanced over at Martin again—but it was hard to tell if the staff's attitude was causing the slow-down or if David just lacked leadership ability. Several staff members had complained to Ed about David, but most of them were whining about him sticking his nose into their business. As far as Ed was concerned, the legacy David had inherited from Joe was mixed at best. And David seemed confused by it all; he spent all of his time trying to get a handle on things, trying too hard to make the staff like him when what he really needed was their respect.

But was he really bad for the Miller Museum? Ed wasn't sure. He wished they had hired someone else, but David was the director now. It was a terrible situation and if he was being completely honest with himself, he would have to take some of the blame.

"Well," he said.

As if he hadn't heard him, Martin said. "Frankly, I don't know quite what to do. Several of us wonder why we didn't give you the job."

As soon as he had said it, Martin wished that he could take it back. He had only confused an already difficult issue.

Ed's mind was racing. He could do this job with his eyes closed; he was sure of it. But the board had wanted someone from outside with more managerial experience than he had, and that's what they had gotten—on paper. Sure, Ed only managed the education programs, which represented just a part of the whole museum, but that didn't mean he couldn't move into the director spot. He had vision, a good way with people, and real drive; he knew he was ready.

He should have pushed the board to make him the director, Ed thought. He would never have gotten into the position David was in; he would have known what to do. But he felt disloyal talking to Martin about David. Where did his loyalty really lie? Was it to David, his boss, who would never even dream that Ed would talk behind his back, especially not to the board chair? Was it to Martin, David's boss, a man who was important in the community but was someone Ed only knew by reputation? Was it to the institution itself, which he loved? If so, what was his responsibility and how could he best fulfill it? Or was it to himself and his family, his ambition? Maybe some of these responsibilities were interconnected. Ed looked at Martin and shifted in his chair.

For Discussion

- What is the situation at the Miller Museum right now?
- What issues have brought the Miller Museum to this point, and could they have been avoided? If yes, how?
- What is, and has been, the role of the board in this situation up to now? Might there have been a different role for the board?
- What should Martin do now?
- When should Martin involve the full board?
- Should board members have known what was going on inside the museum, and how can they find out now?
- How should the board be proceed in this matter?

THE CROWELL PINTER EXHIBITION

Jerome Ethalyn was in the bathroom shaving, half awake and automatically reviewing the workday ahead, when his wife Alice appeared holding a copy of the morning paper.

"I think you should see this, Jerry," she said.

Jerome stared at her image in the mirror, sensing a tightening in his stomach. "What now?" he asked with a sigh. He could see that she was holding the Arts and Culture section and could almost feel Aaron Blake's byline, though he couldn't see it. Jerome wanted to go back to bed, go on vacation, go on sabbatical; he wanted to start the day all over again, because whatever it was, it wasn't going to be good.

For some reason Aaron Blake seemed to have it in for the museum; nobody understood why. From Jerome's first day on the job, the reporter had been a thorn in his side. He could still remember Blake's first column about him:

> The Harder Museum of Art has a new director, Jerome Ethalyn, and by a glance at his background, some would wonder if he's up to the job. Mr. Ethalyn, a small, nervous fellow with a thin moustache, is a graduate of a museum studies program, whatever that might be, and was curator of prints and paper at the Opland Art Museum before coming to us. He may not be overwhelmed by his new responsibilities but he certainly looks like he is. . . .

And the relationship had gone downhill from there. Why? Jerome had never figured it out, and no one on the board seemed to understand it either. Aaron Blake seemed to want to make a difficult job even more difficult. That first article hadn't mentioned Jerome's Ph.D. in American history or the fact that he had raised $15 million to support the Opland's prints and paper collection. It hadn't mentioned that Jerome had been offered the director's job at Opland but only agreed to serve as interim director because he and Alice planned to leave the area eventually; Jerome didn't want to take on such a heavy responsibility and then disappoint the board and staff by leaving. He'd had his eye on the Harder job for a long time; it was his dream job, despite the problems and bad publicity it had had, most of it due to Aaron Blake. It was a wonderful museum, the collections were fabulous and the problems only made the job more interesting.

Jerome took the paper from Alice. It was Aaron Blake's byline all right, under a headline that seemed 3 feet high: "Harder Museum Lines Board Member's Pockets." Jerome frowned. Now what was that supposed to mean? He sat down on the side of the bathtub and began to read.

> We have just learned that noted art collector and, incidentally, Harder Museum of Art board member Stanford Rush will be showing his collection of Crowell Pinter cowboy art at the museum from April to September, in conjunction with an exhibit of Western crafts associated with rural life. Crowell Pinter, recently discovered by the world's art critics and winner of the prestigious Bolton Award, is on a fast track to the top. And with the showing of his collection at the Harder Museum, Stanford Rush will be on a fast track to increase his profits in the art market. The imprimatur of an exhibit at the Harder will make the collection rise in value overnight. Good work, Mr. Rush. It's not everyone who can brand an art investment so quickly—excuse the pun. Wonder if they'd show my art; I have quite a collection, been painting since I was a boy. All I need is the right exhibition venue, and the sky's the limit. How about it, Harder board?

Jerome threw the paper on the floor and finished shaving with a will that left his skin raw; the dapper little moustache went. Alice knew when to leave the room.

In the office, Jerome reached for the telephone before he took off his coat and phoned his board chair, Evette Patterson.

"Have you seen it?" he asked as soon as she answered the telephone.

"Yes," she said. "It's pretty bad. I've called an emergency executive committee meeting."

Jerome nodded. "Have you heard from Stanford?"

"He and Milly left for Arizona this morning, remember?"

"Oh, yes, that's right. At least he isn't here to have to listen to this garbage."

There was a pause on the other end of the line. "Maybe we shouldn't have done it, Jerry," said Evette. "Maybe Aaron's right this time."

"He isn't right. This is ridiculous. Any museum in the country would give an arm and a leg to get hold of Stanford's collection, and we've got it."

"Well, we haven't actually got it; we're just going to exhibit it."

"But he's going to give it to us."

"Has he told you that?"

"No," said Jerome, taken aback. "But we discussed it when the board asked him to become a member, back in August. Do you know something I don't?"

"No, but I know we should never have asked Stanford, or anyone else for that matter, to join the board just because we hope to get something out of it."

"I'm not sure your fellow board members would agree with you."

"Maybe not, but Stanford hardly ever comes to board meetings and when he does he insults just about everyone in the room."

"I'll admit he has been disappointing as a board member, but that isn't really the point. He has an incredible, almost unparalleled collection of Western art and artifacts, and we're going to get it."

"Maybe," Evette said slowly. "Can you join the exec today? We're meeting at my house at 10 o'clock."

"I'll be there."

SARAH FIELDING OPENED THE DOOR before the chimes stopped ringing. She looked somber. "Come on in, Jerome. We're in the conservatory."

Jerome followed her to the sunlit conservatory and joined the group, who already were seated around a large, round glass-topped table, balancing delicate cups on their laps.

"Coffee?" Sarah asked.

Jerome nodded his thanks and looked around the room. Stephen Raynor was there, and Tucker Van Dam, Arlene Brown, Evette, and Sarah. Tucker was leaning forward, the veins in his neck bulging.

"I told you we shouldn't have gone for this exhibit. When he proposed. . . ."

"Actually, Tucker, it was my idea," said Jerome.

Everyone's eyes turned toward him, and Jerome's lip suddenly felt naked without the little moustache. No one seemed to notice. He took a deep breath and continued. "I asked Stanford if we could exhibit the collection; it was a perfect fit with the Western show we were planning. And I was delighted when he said yes. It was only a matter of time before some other museum scooped it up for the first big Pinter show in this area. It was important for us to be first."

"I don't remember discussing it," said Arlene, coldly.

"You were in South Africa, dear," Sarah reminded her. "Taking all those photographs we were so jealous of, remember?"

"Maybe so, but I should have been informed."

"It was in the minutes," said Evette briskly. "Let's not get sidetracked on this. We have a situation here."

"Another Aaron Blake situation," grumbled Tucker, picking up the folded section of newspaper and then slapping it back on the table.

"What should we do?" asked Evette, her dark eyes troubled.

"Kill the bastard," said Stephen. "I swear, if I could get away with it I'd do it."

Jerome, who shared the sentiment, shrugged. "We have to deal with this. Blake has insulted one of our board members, and he has insulted us. He has questioned the integrity of the museum. This isn't just one of his usual rantings; this is a serious issue for us, the kind of thing the wires like to pick up."

"Well, why *did* we do it anyway? Why did we agree, I mean, *ask* to put up his stuff?" Tucker asked, glaring at Jerome.

"It wasn't because we liked him, that's for sure," said Stephen with a little smile. There were weak smiles all around.

Jerome cleared his throat. "No one was trying to increase Stanford's net worth. I recommended to the board that we go ahead with the show, for the reasons I have just mentioned. I don't know if Aaron Blake is ignorant of the importance of this artist, or of the quality of this board, or of the care we all take with the reputation of this museum, or if he just wants to take another swipe at us."

"I could call the paper's editor," said Stephen. "I know him slightly. Blake shouldn't be able to get away with this."

"Been there, done that," sighed Tucker.

"But are we clean?" asked Arlene. "It sounds pretty bad to me from reading the column. I, for one, didn't vote for it."

Evette sighed. "We had a quorum. It was unanimous."

Tucker bristled. "Well, I just voted for it because Stanford was there. I didn't want to insult him."

"Stanford's hard to insult," said Stephen. "He's usually the one doing the insulting. If you didn't want to go forward with this plan, it was your responsibility to vote against it."

"It's still not a bad idea," said Jerome. "Pinter is an important artist, and we are going to be offering the first major showing of his work in the United States. It's a coup for us. The Europeans have been all over him for years."

"But what Blake said about Stanford reaping the benefit," said Arlene. "The man's an oaf. He just might try to sell the collection, like Aaron says."

"No, he won't, and besides, that really isn't the issue," said Jerome. "The board has been accused of feathering the nest of one of its own. The museum has been accused of participating in a scam."

"Jerome's right," said Evette. "First, we have to look at the issue calmly. Quarreling among ourselves will get us nowhere. Then we have to decide what we are going to do, why we are going to do it, how we are going to do it, and what we expect and want the outcome to be. We also should talk about how to prevent such a situation from arising again. I need you all to give me your best thinking, now."

For Discussion

- Did the board make an irresponsible decision?
- Did the board make an informed decision?
- What is the relationship between the CEO and the board chair?
- Does this situation represent a real conflict of interest or a perceived conflict of interest?
- How could this situation have been avoided?
- What should they do now?
- What do you notice about this board culture?
- What do you notice about the management style of this CEO?

A CAPITAL EXPERIENCE

Bob Martinez pulled his car into the space marked "Director, Foley Museum" and turned off the engine. He sat for a moment, both hands still on the steering wheel, thinking about the weeks and months ahead, and the advisability of continuing with the Capital Campaign. He had spent most of the night before going over the figures provided by Ellie Stuart, the VP for finance, and he was depressed. Suddenly, he got out of the car, slamming the door shut. This was no time for fatigue, depression, worry, confusion, or any other useless emotions. It was a time for decision.

Of course, they could still stop the Capital Campaign, which had not yet gone into its public phase. But the museum needed money desperately. The building, though elegant, with its orange tile roof and stately columns, was large and old, and had serious deferred maintenance and safety issues. In addition, the exhibits were out of date. New exhibitions techniques, an experiential focus, well-documented research on different learning styles of visitors, conservation needs—everything argued for a complete redo if the museum was to compete successfully for the leisure time of modern visitors.

Bob tugged on the heavy metal side door of the museum and stepped inside the cool, dark hallway, nodding to the guard as he walked to the elevator.

"Morning, Jeb," he said.

"Morning, Dr. Martinez," the elderly man answered.

Bob loved this place. He loved its smell and its traditions, but he knew it had to change. He sighed, wondering for the 100th time in the last several weeks whether he should have taken the job at the Foley Museum in the first place. He had been happy enough in the East, but the opportunity to direct a larger, more venerable institution in the Southwest, closer to his family and his spiritual roots, had been a siren's song he couldn't resist.

He rode the elevator to the fourth floor and walked briskly to his office. His secretary, Belinda Matthews, was already at her large oak desk. "Good morning, Bob," she said with a smile. She handed him a square stack of pink slips of paper, with an apologetic look. "Lots of calls yesterday," she said.

With a grimace, he thumbed through the pink slips. "Had to go pay my respects to the legislature. You never know when they may cut us in for some special project—or cut us off." He smiled weakly. "Stopped off at Allied Corporation, too, on my way home. There may be something there."

His director of development, Allison Lomax, had called, and there were several messages from Henry Washington, director of programs. "Would you call Allison and Henry and see if they can come up for a meeting in a half hour, and see if Ellie's free. We need to do some serious talking about the Capital Campaign."

Belinda nodded. "Will do," she said, and picked up the telephone receiver.

Bob spread the pink slips across his desk, sighed, and leaned back in his chair, rubbing his eyes. He was tired. He knew he should call Bruce Dolant, the chairman of the board of trustees, but he didn't feel up to it. He had discussed the board's role in fund raising with Bruce before and had gotten nowhere. But one thing was certain. Bob Martinez could not do this by himself. Even with the able assistance of Allison and her small staff, he could not do it.

The Capital Campaign was a real stretch for the Foley. Not much fund raising had been done in the past. And when the former director launched the campaign he had little understanding of what it meant and had done virtually no planning for it; he only knew that the institution needed money. Bob knew the institution needed money, too, and surely the board did as well. He got a cold, hard feeling in the pit of his stomach every time he thought about the money. He was pretty sure he had been hired to raise it—$20 million on a virtually non-existent base of support, with a board that was lukewarm at best on the subject of fund raising.

Belinda stuck her head around the door. "They'll all be here, Bob," she said.

He nodded absent-mindedly and thanked her.

To their credit, the board had raised $5 million among themselves. They were generous, and they were committed. But they seemed to think that they had done their part and that now it was up to him and Allison. He could cheerfully have strangled his predecessor for putting him in this situation, but Neil Osmond had retired and moved to South Dakota, where one of his daughters lived. Clearly Bob would be the scapegoat if the money was not raised. Whom else could the trustees blame?

But Bob knew he couldn't raise the money without them. He was fairly new in town; the museum would be changing radically in a relatively conservative community; and there was no donor base to speak of. Until now the museum had survived on the small endowment left by Max Foley, the proceeds from an exceedingly popular annual special event, ticket sales, restaurant and shop revenues, and memberships. But even while Neil was still here, revenues had flattened and even begun to decline, not that they had ever been adequate support for the museum. Much that should have been done long ago had been put off. How had the place gotten in such a sorry state?

Bob was startled out of his reveries by the buzzer on his desk. "Yes?" he said.

"They're here," said Belinda.

"Thanks. Send them in." Bob stood up to greet the key members of his senior staff. He had counted on these three people from his first days on the job, and they had never let him down.

Allison entered the room first, trim and elegant in a dark gray suit and white silk blouse. She was followed by Henry, who looked casually hip as usual. They were unusually silent and moved toward the empty chairs facing Bob's desk almost automatically. They had been expecting something for weeks, they just weren't sure what was about to happen. A few minutes later, Ellie Jackson burst into the room, out of breath and red faced.

"Sorry to be late," she said. "The elevator's stuck. I took the stairs."

"It's good for you," said Henry, smiling as she threw him a murderous look.

"You're not late," said Bob, "Allison and Henry just got here." He looked at the three of them. Then, frowning, he said, "I've been thinking that we should drop the Capital Campaign."

The room was silent. He could see that they wanted to look at each other, but all three kept their eyes firmly on his face.

Finally Henry spoke up. "I know it's been tough, Bob, but we need this money desperately." He raised an eyebrow and looked over at Ellie. "Even the elevator doesn't work now."

"He's right, Bob," said Ellie. "Have you had a chance to look at the numbers I gave you last night and the list of deferred maintenance items? It's staggering. Even the Capital Campaign won't solve all our problems."

Allison leaned forward, her face tense and pale. "I agree with both of you, of course. But where's the money going to come from?"

"We're in a fund-raising campaign, aren't we?" asked Henry. "That's where the money's supposed to come from."

"Henry, you know it isn't as easy as that. The Foley has never really done any serious fund raising and, because of that, we have hardly any donors."

Ellie tucked a strand of hair behind her ear. "But the board itself has given us $5 million dollars," she said. "I think that's pretty spectacular. The Foley has never had that much money at one time."

Bob hesitated and then said, "Yes, but there is $15 million more to be raised."

"And you can't get the board to assume the responsibility, am I right?" asked Henry.

"Right," sighed Bob. "How did you know?"

"I worked for two other museums before I came to the Foley. It was the same for them. You're just lucky the board members came through themselves. Sometimes that doesn't happen either."

"I know," said Bob. "We have a really good board. I like each and every one of them, and they are all committed to the Foley's future. They just don't see fund raising as one of their responsibilities. They want me to do it. It's what they hired me for."

Ellie crossed her arms. "Didn't you talk about the campaign when they interviewed you?"

"Sure, we did. But I assumed that a board as active as this one seemed to be, with the financial resources it obviously had, would know that I wouldn't be able to raise that kind of money, or even come close to it, without them. I'm not a peer. The people we have to ask for money don't want to hear from me, or they want what I say validated by one of their own and they want that person along on the call."

Henry nodded. "What does Bruce say?"

Bob sighed. "Bruce doesn't really engage the question. I don't think he knows what to do, and he is probably no more anxious to be out fund raising than anyone else on the board. Allison," he said, "you always did the fund raising alone, didn't you?"

"Such as it was. We had the Springding fund raiser each year."

Henry interrupted. "Wasn't there some problem with that last year?"

Allison nodded. "Sally Randolph was the chair of the committee, and she, well, I don't know how to describe it. She was abusive to me, the rest of the staff, and even some of her fellow board members, and she wouldn't share any information with the rest of the committee. It was awful. Half the committee resigned."

"Why didn't someone do something about it?" asked Ellie.

"Well, clearly I couldn't," Allison said. "Mrs. Randolph is one of the most influential people in this community, and her husband is president of National Bank." She sighed. "I talked to Bruce about it, but he didn't want to get involved and he said the board wouldn't want to either. No one wanted to offend Mrs. Randolph. They all have to get along together. It's about a lot more than this museum."

"But it cost us, in members and revenue, right?" asked Henry.

"Yes," said Allison, "and it will be a long time before I can get any volunteers to work on a project like that again. But back to Bob's question about our past fund-raising efforts, I worked hard at increasing membership and wrote proposals to foundations and a few corporations. We were more successful than we deserved to be. But I didn't have the connections to the movers and shakers in town. And even if I had, as you said, they wouldn't want to talk to me; they want to talk to a member of the board, someone they know and trust. Sure, I got some gifts of $5,000, even a couple at $10,000. But we're talking about raising $15 million. I can't do that without the help of the board."

"I can't understand why they don't know that," said Ellie slowly.

"Well, they don't," said Bob, "and I've got to decide to either shut down the campaign or try to get the board to work with me."

Allison leaned forward. "You have to get the board to work with us. If you don't, nothing will ever change."

"You're talking about a big culture shift here, Allison," said Henry, sharply. "These people have done a lot for this museum, and they have given a lot of their own money."

"I understand that, Henry, but I also know that we are dependent on the board for our financial resources. If they don't take on their fund-raising responsibility, and aren't challenged on it, the culture will never change and the Foley Museum will slowly die."

Bob nodded. "I agree with Allison. I've got to do something."

"But what can you do? You've already tried talking to Bruce," said Ellie.

"What about going to the executive committee?" said Henry. "Bruce is a great guy, but he's not a very strong leader. Maybe one of the others would be able to do something."

Bob shrugged. "I don't think that's appropriate; maybe I wasn't strong enough in making my points."

"You could be right, but even if you said it perfectly, would they really hear you?"

Bob shrugged. "The thing is, either I make my point with Bruce and risk a serious rift with him and probably the rest of the board, or I don't do it, the campaign is a failure, and I get blamed for it. Either way, I'll probably get fired."

"You could cancel the campaign," said Allison reluctantly, "I suppose."

Bob shook his head. "I can't even cancel the campaign without board approval, and I'm not sure they would understand. This has to be hit head on. And the truth is, I'm not sure how to do it. They are, after all, my bosses. I can't order them around."

"What about having a big meeting," suggested Henry, leaning back in his chair, "the kind that includes our partners, like Big Brothers/Big Sisters, La Casa, the schools we work with. You could bill it as a general brainstorming meeting. It might put pressure on the board."

"It could backfire," said Ellie.

"Or not work at all," answered Allison.

"Can't know until you try," said Henry.

They sat quietly, thinking about all of these things, but not saying anything. None of them knew how to move the board either. Finally Bob broke the silence.

"I need a little time to think about this. Maybe I'm wrong, but I believe this problem has the potential to end my career here." He looked at them, his dark eyes serious and troubled. "I would like each of you to think about it, too. It would help me if we could meet again tomorrow morning, same time, same place, and talk about this once more. I need your advice."

The others nodded. "Of course, Bob."

"Sure."

"See you tomorrow."

One by one they filed out of the office, looking glum. When Belinda peeked around the office door she saw Bob standing at the window with his hands in his pockets and deep in thought.

For Discussion
- What could the museum have done to avoid this problem?
- What could the board have done to avoid this problem?
- What are the respective roles of the CEO and board chair in this case?
- What should Bob do if Bruce refuses to confront his board?
- What should Bruce do if he confronts the board and its members refuse to fund raise?
- Should the campaign be cancelled? If yes, what should the museum and board do to address the critical need for funding? If no, how should the museum and board proceed?
- What can be learned from this situation?

WHOSE MUSEUM?

Eloise Drew hurried into the River Run Café and looked around the small restaurant. Sandra Nichols was not there yet, thank goodness. Sandra had just gotten back from Mexico, was it yesterday? A group of friends, all of them on the Waters Mill House Museum board, had taken a trip together, just for fun, Sandra had said. She was probably still feeling a little jet lagged, but she wouldn't have forgotten. Sandra didn't forget.

"Table for one, Madam?" asked a waiter.

"No, there will be two of us. Could we have a table outside on the patio? It's such a lovely day."

"Certainly, Madam," he said, "Come with me." He pointed to a small, wrought-iron table by the rose bushes. "Will this do?" he asked.

"Yes, thank you," said Eloise, "it's very nice."

"And your friend, Madam? How shall I recognize her?"

Eloise smiled, amused to hear the patrician Sandra Nichols described as her friend. Sandra was far too elegant, far too poised, and far too conscious of her own social position to ever consider Eloise her friend, but it was a nice thought.

"She's rather tall and thin, very elegant, with short white hair and blue eyes. She'll come in like she owns the place." Eloise felt a little guilty about that last comment, but it did describe Sandra and it would help the waiter recognize her immediately.

Ever since Eloise had joined the board of the Waters Museum, she had watched Sandra, so poised, so cool, and so domineering, and wondered how the poor director, Bill Starling, managed to keep from trembling in front of her. Fortunately Sandra wasn't the board chair, so he probably didn't have to interact with her too much, but she was the founder of the Waters Museum and she never seemed to be satisfied with anything. And Daniel Winters, the board chair, was not the person to challenge Sandra on anything, not directly anyway. Although he had allowed that one issue to come before the board while she was away.

Eloise's stomach was in knots. She was never comfortable in Sandra's presence and couldn't imagine why she'd been invited to lunch today. The two women scarcely knew each other. Eloise pulled her compact out of her purse and examined her face. Not much she could do there, she thought. She pushed at her hair but the springy curls bounced away from her hand and back into their random chaos; to someone like Sandra she probably seemed unkempt and impossibly young.

Aside from whatever Sandra wanted to discuss, something else was nagging at Eloise, saying, you need to tell her what happened at the board meeting. Eloise suddenly felt guilty; Sandra was going to be furious when she found out. No one on the board knew Eloise was having lunch with Sandra; they would all be as surprised as she was herself she suspected. She wasn't a part of Sandra's social set, not even close, part of the board's attempts to diversify actually, she was pretty sure of that. Not that she couldn't hold her own in any group, but Eloise felt that she was the wrong messenger for the news Sandra was going to have to hear. On the other hand, if she didn't say anything today, when it all came out Sandra would realize that Eloise had kept it from her on purpose. Either way she was going to get killed.

While Sandra was away, the board, voting on a motion Bill had presented, decided to close down the original Waters Museum exhibit on the migration of people into the region, the one they called their permanent exhibit. It was old and out of date and, in truth, not completely accurate. Although some of the artifacts were interesting, Bill said, it was an embarrassment; whole groups of people were unrepresented and the museum had received a lot of complaints about it. There were no plans to reopen the exhibit any time soon, or at any time as far as Eloise could tell; there just wasn't any money to redo an entire gallery. Bill's point had been very simple and made a lot of sense. Their story was an industrial story set in an old mill town. The peopling of the area was an important topic, something anyone coming into the museum would expect to see. Right now it was a dreary exhibit that did not begin to represent the diversity of the region. No one ever looked at it any more, and they should probably all be thankful for that. Something had to be done about it—it should be their strongest exhibit. In the meantime the old exhibit, which was truly an embarrassment, had to go.

It wasn't all that surprising that the motion had passed. After all, Sandra and her strongest supporters—all original trustees and still on the board—were in

Mexico, and the board had recently added several newer, younger members, like Eloise herself, more representative of the people who lived in the valley. There had been more than enough board members for a quorum, and the motion had passed unanimously.

"My dear," Sandra's voice pierced through Eloise's thoughts, and she jumped. "Oh, I am sorry, did I scare you?" Sandra's voice held just a note of, what was it?

"You didn't scare me, Sandra, I was deep in thought, that's all." Eloise reached up and smoothed her hair but she could feel it spring back uncooperatively. "How was your trip?"

'Absolutely wonderful. How have things been here, and at the museum?"

"Oh, fine, just fine."

"Well, I have great news for the board, but since you're the one I'm seeing first, you're the one who will hear it first. I've bought a tapestry from one of the most famous haciendas in Mexico; it's Spanish really, dates from the 16th century and has been in the family's collection for generations. I had to pay a pretty penny for it, I can tell you, but it will be perfect in the front hall of the museum."

Eloise looked at her in surprise. "The front hall? I thought we were going to turn that into an introductory exhibit on the museum."

"Well, we are dear, but this won't hurt anything; we can hang it on the wall for that matter. It's so bright and colorful, simply gorgeous. It'll be the first thing you see when you enter the museum. It's so lively—we need a little livening up don't you think?"

Eloise swallowed. "I'm sure it is, Sandra. But what does it have to do with the museum?"

"Nothing really, I suppose," Sandra sighed as if the question was just too tiresome. "But it is so lovely. Shouldn't people who live here, people who can't get to Mexico, be able to see such a perfect artifact, one that's so old?" Not expecting an answer, Sandra picked up her menu and began to read down the list of the day's specials. Then she smiled over at Eloise.

"Tell me about the board meeting, my dear. I was so sorry to miss it but there just wasn't any choice. We had a certain window for this trip, and we took it."

Eloise flushed. Stupidly she had thought she might be able to keep the conversation away from the museum.

"Oh, it was fine," she said, staring at her own menu with great concentration.

"Anything interesting happen?" asked Sandra. "Anything I should know about to prepare me for my meeting with Bill. I have a meeting with him scheduled for next week; did I tell you?"

"No," said Eloise, surprised.

"Actually that's why I invited you to lunch. I wanted to talk to you about Bill. But first, let's order." Sandra signaled to the waiter. "And then you tell me about the board meeting, and I'll tell you what I have planned for my meeting with Bill."

Eloise swallowed and nodded.

They ordered lunch and as soon as the waiter had left the table, Sandra leaned forward. "Now, about the board meeting. How did Daniel handle himself?"

What a surprising question, Eloise thought. Daniel might be a little weak as chair, but he always handled himself well. She sensed that Sandra didn't like him much, but Eloise couldn't figure out what the problem was; Daniel was perfectly nice.

"Oh, he was fine. We moved through the agenda pretty quickly."

"Was anything special on the agenda?" Sandra smiled and leaned even closer.

Eloise felt trapped. "Nothing much," she began, then forced herself to go on. "Oh, except," she said as casually as she could, "we did vote to close the permanent gallery."

"What?" Sandra sat up, her blue eyes cold. "What do you mean you voted to close the permanent gallery?"

"It's very old and out of date; it wasn't representing the museum well. That consultant that was here last month, the one Bill brought in to look at the collections, suggested it. He said it was unrepresentative and inaccurate."

"That's ridiculous. It has some of the best things in the museum in it. I designed it myself. That exhibit is the museum; it stays."

Eloise looked up. "We voted to close it, Sandra."

"But I wasn't there. Carol and Barbara, Frank, Mike, and Jason—they were all with me."

"We had a quorum."

"We'll see about that." Sandra was fuming. "This is exactly why I wanted you to meet me. This is a perfect example of how Bill tries to undermine me all the time. I told him not to hire that consultant; it was a pure waste of money. And now this. He would never have dared to pull such a stunt if I'd been here. The truth is, he doesn't really understand what this museum is all about, and I want him gone. It is our right to hire and fire the museum director. We discussed this in great detail on our trip, and we're all agreed. Bill has to go."

Eloise cleared her throat. "This is a surprise," she said, hating herself for the banal comment, but it reflected how she felt.

"Yes, well, I wanted to ask you for your support. It will come up for a vote at the next board meeting."

"Does Bill know about this?"

"Not yet," said Sandra dryly, "but he will after my meeting with him. I'm planning to talk about this with most of the new board members before then. You're the first."

Eloise looked at the other people quietly eating their lunch, at the flowers and the way the sun slanted in over the hedge. She straightened in her chair and looked at Sandra directly. It was a shame she had to take all this lovely peace and throw it away. "I'm sorry Sandra," she said, "I could never support something like that. I think Bill is doing a fine job." She decided not to ask why Daniel wasn't the one meeting with Bill, if such a meeting was even appropriate.

"How can you say that? He maneuvered all of you to get rid of the permanent gallery while I was away; he knew I would oppose that. Last year he refused to launch a capital campaign for a new wing, and we need that new wing. If we expand, and I know just the architect, we'll have more visitors."

The logic of this argument escaped Eloise, who believed that the board should pay attention to the things the museum was doing now rather than start anything new. The board seldom talked about really important things, like its vision for the future or the museum's priorities.

"I'm sorry, Sandra," Eloise repeated, "I won't support you in this."

Sandra stared at her across the table, her icy blue eyes cold and hard. Then she picked up her purse and pushed back her chair. "There's nothing more to say, I guess," she said. "But I am disappointed in you. I thought you understood the ideas behind this museum."

The waiter approached the table with their salads. "She coming back?" he asked, watching Sandra as she stalked away. Eloise shook her head. "No, I don't think so."

He placed the salads on the table. "Will you be staying?" he asked.

Eloise nodded and leaned back in her chair. The next board meeting was going to be a doozy, or maybe not. Nobody ever said what he was really thinking; it was conceivable that Sandra and her supporters would prevail. Would Eloise dare to defy that cabal when they were all seated around the same table?

This was a big issue; it ought to bring everyone out of the woodwork and then she wouldn't be alone, she was sure of it. But if she *was* alone, would she speak up? Everyone seemed to be a little afraid of Sandra for some reason. The most important thing was to keep the discussion professional. The worst that could happen to the Waters Museum was a lot of screaming and shouting at board meetings and excessive lobbying—Eloise was sure that was what Sandra would do—inside and outside the museum. It either was going to be ugly or everyone would pretend there had been a terrible misunderstanding. If that happened Eloise would have to leave the board; she would have no respect for any of them.

For Discussion

- What is the situation at the Waters Museum? Describe the board, the board chair, and the CEO.
- Could this situation have been avoided? If yes, how? If no, what should happen next and who should be involved?
- Was the board justified in proceeding as it did? What was gained by proceeding as it did? What was lost?
- How should this situation be handled now?
- What is the most important lesson to be drawn from this case?

DOES ONE PLUS ONE = TWO, OR TROUBLE?

The tall glass windows of the Langley Museum of Native American Culture and Regional History looked out onto the empty parking lot. The summer twilight made the sky look gray, and the air was quiet and peaceful. Doris Cook enjoyed being in the museum after most people had gone home and the phones were quiet. It was a good time to get work done. And there was plenty to do because the Langley Museum's City Advisory Board was going to meet tomorrow, and its Foundation Board would meet following day. Two boards, two agendas, two different sets of issues.

Doris turned away from the windows and walked back to her desk. She had been the museum's director for three years, but only now was she starting to understand the many layers of personalities and issues that had contributed to the museum's development in the past and continued to direct its course in the present. Twelve years ago Bessie Langley had left to the city her vast collection of artifacts, all related to the region and its earliest inhabitants, along with enough money to build a museum to house them. It was a wonderful museum, and Doris was happy to be there. There were so many wonderful opportunities to work with the community; help the local residents (and what a diverse group of people they were!) and the many visitors understand how the area had developed over time; and to create a sense of pride about the region's significant and colorful history, developing the story right up to the present.

Although Doris had been in the museum field for more than 20 years, she had never worked with two boards before, and it was a challenge. But she didn't have a choice, and she had to make the most of it. And the two boards were so different. Doris looked at the agenda for the City Advisory Board meeting and read down the list of issues to be approved: the budget, maintenance of the physical plant, the Earth Day festival in April, requests for a curator and funds for the oral history project, and the renovation of the permanent gallery. Doris knew the board didn't have any power to ensure that she got the money; it was only an advisory body anyway, and she reported to the city manager. But the board members were influential people who could help her lobby for funds within city government. If only they would. What they really wanted to do was plan the museum's exhibitions and programs and make sure that she did everything correctly, "by the book," which was a bit of a problem since, of course, there was no book.

Since the museum received most of its money from the city, no one could deny that the city should play a major role in the institution, but that didn't make things any easier. The eight members of the City Advisory Board had been appointed by Mayor Caldwell, and Doris was lucky that they were as good as they were. They were people the mayor wanted to honor with an administration appointment of some sort, but they weren't big enough players to have a significant role in one of the more important divisions. The museum was perfect for the mayor's political supporters; they couldn't do much harm, or so the mayor thought, and the museum was an interesting place. The board members saw themselves as representatives of the city, whose job was to make sure that the leadership (Doris) was honest and that the museum didn't do anything controversial. They referred to themselves as watchdogs, and went over all the museum's plans with Doris before they were finalized and approved any new programs. At their last meeting, they'd had a long discussion about the renewal of the permanent galleries, a costly endeavor, but in the end they had approved the project.

On the other hand, the Foundation Board had been established six years ago in response to the museum's need for an independent 501(c)3 group to raise additional funds, since it was obvious that the institution needed more money than the city could, or would, provide. However, most of the foundation's members were in no position to raise the kind of money that the museum needed. They managed the Earth Day special event and the museum's shop, and they held bake sales and organized historical tours of the city to generate revenue. They raised about $40,000 a year, not an insignificant amount but nowhere near the $6 to $8 million that Doris projected would be needed over the next several years.

Doris looked at the agenda for the Foundation Board's meeting, which listed her request for $1.5 million to redo the permanent gallery. In a way she hated to do present it to them; for one thing they would be angry that they had not had any input into the project, and even if they had, she knew they couldn't raise the money. Yes, the Foundation Board members were devoted to the museum, but they were archeologists, retired teachers, and a few collectors and hobbyists—not people of serious means or with serious connections to the local community, much less the region. They wanted nothing more than the museum's (and Doris's) success, and as supporters and cheerleaders they could not be beat; but as a fund-raising arm? Still, who else could she turn to? The members of the City Advisory Board had made it clear that they would not do any fund raising; they were the city's eyes and ears, and they thought of themselves as museum planners—and no more.

Most difficult for Doris was that the two boards did not get along with one another at all. They never met together, and although she did her best to bridge the communication gap by telling each group what the other was doing, it never seemed to be enough. One board was always surprised about something and usually wasn't happy about it. For example, a few days earlier Fred Chamberlain, the city board's chairman, had found out that last year the foundation's contribution dropped from $40,000 to $32,000. He seemed to think that the foundation members had done it on purpose, when Doris knew that terrible weather had ruined the Earth Day event and the shop had been closed for three months while Molly Whitley had her surgery. But Fred had gone on and on about it, insisting that he would bring it up for discussion at tomorrow's board meeting. Doris couldn't see the point, since the city board had no power over the foundation; all that would do was stir everyone up.

And she had scarcely hung up the telephone when Betsy Chelinoff, president of the Foundation Board, called about the agenda for her meeting.

"What do you mean, redo the permanent galleries? And for $1.5 million? We've never heard about any of this."

"The museum board approved the plans, Betsy," said Doris, before she could stop herself.

"Well, of course they approved the plans; they always approve the plans. Why not? They just sit over there approving and then expect us to raise money for things we know absolutely nothing about. That really makes me mad, Doris; it makes all of us very mad. Why don't they get off their duffs and raise a little money themselves? They're the ones that make all the plans."

"They're a little constrained in what they can do in terms of fund raising," said Doris. "As city employees. . . ."

"They're not city employees," snapped Betsy in exasperation. "Jack Natter runs Sarah's Deli downtown. Brian has the Ford dealership, as you well know. And Fred, why, he's a divorce lawyer. They could help. And *we* should be part of any planning the museum does. How else are we going to have a say about what we're raising money for?"

Doris actually agreed with Betsy on this, but the City Advisory Board was opposed to it, seeing planning as its prerogative.

She put both agendas back down on her desk and leaned back in her chair. She wasn't looking forward to either meeting. Didn't the boards see how destructive this was for the museum?

For Discussion

- What are the pros and cons of having two boards for the Langley Museum?
- How could two boards, both focused on the museum's success, have developed such a distant relationship, and what must change for their service to the museum to be productive?
- Can the CEO initiate a change in the way the two boards operate? If yes, how? If no, who can and how should they proceed?
- Should the city be involved in this matter? If yes, how, who should solicit its assistance, and for what?
- What is the first step to be taken?

THE SURPRISE

"I know you're busy planning today's Chamber of Commerce speech, Patricia, but Mrs. Whitman is here."

Surprised, Patricia Spaulding looked up from her notes and then nodded. Even if the museum were on fire, she could hardly refuse to see the board chair. As director of the Stone Town Museum of Natural History, her relationship with Stephanie Whitman should be important and close. It was neither, and Patricia regretted it.

"Do you know what she wants?" Patricia asked, pushing the notes of last night's board meeting to one side.

Her assistant shrugged. "She didn't tell me, but she seems excited."

Oh, Lord. Patricia's heart sank. Stephanie probably had another idea, one more thing for the staff to do. Didn't the woman realize there was a limit? Did she understand, for that matter did anyone else on the board understand, how much they were doing already?

"Send her in," she said with a sigh, gathering her strength. A glance at the clock told her that it was only 10 o'clock in the morning. Why did she suddenly feel so tired?

"Patricia," called Stephanie from the doorway. "How are you?" She hurried across the room, the long silk scarf draped around her neck floating behind her.

"You look wonderful, Stephanie," Patricia said truthfully.

Stephanie's gray hair was almost white and her face was lined and heavily, carefully, made up, but she had the figure of a much younger woman and the energy of a teenager. This morning she was bubbling over about something; there was a sparkle in her eyes that Patricia hadn't seen before. It worried her.

"You'll never guess what just happened, my dear."

"What?" asked Patricia, wishing she didn't have to know, not when the day was so young and she was already so tired.

"Well, I was a bit disturbed last night that there was so little interest in my suggestion that we attach a small petting zoo to our exhibit on the natural world."

"I can understand that; I know you wanted it," said Patricia. "But Stephanie, we're really not set up for live animals here and besides, that's not exactly what "Natural World" is about."

"Well, it should be. Farm animals are part of the natural world, aren't they?" asked Stephanie. "All those frogs and tadpoles and wild things are just fine. But I grew up on a farm, and I know how important farm animals are to, well, to just about everything."

A small cold shiver worked its way through Patricia. The last thing she wanted was a disagreement with Stephanie; it just wouldn't do. Stone Town's last director had been fired over clashes with the board. Besides, Patricia liked Stephanie very much, though as a board chair she was hopeless.

"I guess," she said, warmly. "It's just that no one could figure out where we would get the money to renovate the museum so it could house live animals. Besides, the costs of sustaining the exhibit would be sky high, as you said yourself."

Stephanie patted her hair and gave Patricia a self-satisfied smile. "Not to worry. I've found a donor."

"*What?*" Patricia was unaware that she had jumped up. She cleared her throat and, in a calmer voice, asked, "What did you say, Stephanie?"

"I've found a donor for the petting zoo, my dear. Bradley Portman, who used to own the Federal Cattle and Milk conglomerate, has given me a pledge for $500,000. The zoo is ours."

Patricia groaned. She had been planning to ask Bradley Portman to support the museum's next major exhibition or the theater they needed so badly. She took a deep breath. "But Stephanie, we don't have the staff to care for live animals, and even if we did, they don't fit in the exhibit."

Stephanie looked at Patricia in amazement. "Bradley Portman. Patricia, we've been trying to get to him for years."

"But not for this."

"I thought you'd be pleased." Stephanie moved the strap of her purse more tightly against her shoulder. "Once the board hears about this, they'll be thrilled. That consultant said, find out what the donor is interested in and match it with the museum's needs, and that's just what I did."

Patricia could feel a hot prickling sensation at the base of her neck. "This isn't one of the museum's priorities, Stephanie. We went through a very thoughtful process last year listing all of the museum's initiatives in priority order. This wasn't even on the list."

"I knew Bradley wouldn't be interested in those things; I had a feeling the petting zoo would get him going, and it did."

"Stephanie," Patricia sat back down. "We are not going to have a petting zoo at the Stone Town Museum. It just isn't appropriate. I wish you had told me you were going to Bradley Portman. I've been trying to meet him ever since I took this job. I'm sure I could have interested him in some of the programs we have planned."

Stephanie looked puzzled, and a little angry. "What do you mean we're not going to do the petting zoo? I asked for the money, and he gave it to me. This would be a personal embarrassment for me, not to mention the museum. Bradley is very influential around here."

"Precisely why I wanted to meet him," said Patricia. "I've been trying to get an appointment with him for weeks."

"Why didn't you ask me?"

With a twinge of guilt Patricia thought about why: it was a call she wanted to make on her own with her own agenda and no wild cards. She had deliberately decided not to invite Stephanie to any meeting with Portman, even though she knew the two were acquainted. Patricia had just figured that sooner or later she would get to him, and when she did, she would be ready.

"Why didn't you ask me?" Stephanie asked again. "Oh, this is so embarrassing. Why didn't you tell me you wanted to see him? I could have introduced you."

"Why didn't you tell me you were going to see him, Stephanie?" Patricia asked in turn, irritation creeping into her voice. "I can't have board members going out and doing things on their own."

Stephanie paused a moment. She had known that Patricia didn't like the zoo project, and she'd had a feeling that Bradley would. Bradley was hers, and she was going to deliver him. She straightened her back.

"I'm the chair of the board, not a mere board member, and I can't have the museum's director deliberately trying to keep me out of important meetings. If you didn't tell me you wanted to see him, it can only be because you didn't want me there."

Stephanie turned and hurried toward the door. She paused and turned back. "I will not be embarrassed. Not in front of my board and not in front of my community. You figure out what you're going to do about this, and let me know." With that, she stormed out of the room.

The outer office door slammed loudly. Patricia flinched.

Stephanie hurried toward her car.

"Stephanie!"

She turned, and saw Henry Sessing walking toward her.

"Where are you off to?" he asked. "I have a meeting with Patricia. If I'd known you were going to be here, we could have had lunch."

"You have a meeting with Patricia?"

He nodded, running his hand over his bald spot. "She called me last night, after the board meeting, and asked me to come in."

"Do you know what she wants?"

"I think she wants to talk about that new staff position they want in the development department." He sighed. "I don't know why you made me the chair of that committee anyway."

"What new staff position?"

Henry frowned. "She mentioned it last night, remember, when we were talking about the possibility of a Capital Campaign. She said they couldn't do it without another person in development."

"I thought we decided not to do the Capital Campaign."

Henry shrugged. "The museum needs real money, and I think they need it pretty badly."

"I know nothing about this, Henry," Stephanie said. "May I come to the meeting with you?"

For Discussion

- What are the real issues here?
- In hindsight, what problems brought the museum to this spot, and what could have prevented this situation from arising?
- What can be done now?
- What are the appropriate roles for the CEO, board, and board chair in this situation? Who should take the lead? Why?
- What can be done to prevent a similar situation in the future?

DOES BETTER MEAN BIGGER?

"Lillian, I need to see you," said Nicholas Wentworth, director of the Farmington Isles Historical Society. His grip on the telephone was tight and his stomach clenched like a fist. Nicholas's relationship with his board chair wasn't all that he had hoped it would be when he took the job. Lillian was jealous of her prerogatives as chair, and she wanted no interference with the board's discussion of museum issues. Worse, she seemed to need little information about what those issues might be and liked to linger over discussions the way one might over a good cup of coffee, refilling it every time it got cold. But it was more than that. While she was, toward him at least, spiteful, she wasn't very forceful. The board operated like a group of friends. Real work was the last thing on their minds.

"What is it, Nicholas?" she said. He could hear her pencil tapping beside the telephone. "You'll have to tell me over the phone. I'm about to leave for the country."

Great. Another trip to her country place. In the summer Lillian was almost impossible to see.

"We need a board retreat to discuss where the society is headed, Lillian. We are at a real crossroads and I'm concerned. One of my colleagues told me about a planning consultant in our area who is supposed to be very good. I want to hire her."

"What on earth are you concerned about," she asked, her tone bringing a flush to his face. "Everything's just fine."

"No, Lillian, everything is not fine. Last night the board voted to buy the building next to the museum for $5 million."

"I'm aware of that Nicholas. I was at the board meeting." Her tone was patient but obviously so.

"We need to revisit that decision," Nicholas said.

"The board *voted*, Nicholas."

"I know. I just don't think they had all the facts."

"That's your job, isn't it?"

"Well, yes, but I never believed for a minute they would approve it. I only addressed my fund-raising concerns; I said nothing about the strategic development of the museum."

"What strategic development?"

"That's just it; we're moving forward without any plan, without having even the most superficial discussion about our priorities."

"And you need a consultant to help with that?"

"The consultant will act as a facilitator and make sure we stay on track," Nicholas explained. "We have some big decisions to make. The most obvious one is, what is the historical society's future? Where do we want to see ourselves 10 years from now? What are our priorities? Do we even need the building, and if we do, what for? And then there is the fund raising. Sure, we could expand our programming, and the museum's attendance has grown tremendously the last several years. But the size of the staff hasn't grown, our fund-raising efforts haven't grown, and if we take on this responsibility, we will have to change in some very significant ways. It's like the domino that touches the one next to it, which touches the one next to it, and so on. Each move we're making has far-reaching consequences, and I don't think we've discussed them enough."

"Why didn't you bring this up last night if you were so worried?"

"I tried, but no one seemed to understand what I was saying. We shouldn't do this, or at least we can't do this without real change inside the organization."

"Are you saying you don't think we're up to the task?"

Nicholas paused. "That's not what I mean, Lillian. The historical society has been doing a great job. We have been very successful; museums across the country see us as a model because of the way we serve our visitors. We have very diverse audiences, increasingly so, and our programs bring them back time and again; the programs are educational and enjoyable, even entertaining and people love them."

"That's why we have to grow," Lillian said. "There isn't room in the building for all that we want to do."

"That is completely true. I don't disagree with that at all. I'm just not sure the board understands all the ramifications of the decision it made last night. We'll be a new museum."

"Yes?"

"It will take a lot more money, a lot more. It's not just the capital costs, there will be considerable new costs for operations." He was going off track again; he had to get the conversation back to the real issue. "We need to think about what we are as a museum and what we want to be. We need to plan our direction in a thoughtful, considered, strategic way."

"Nicholas, we all know where we want to go, even you. We don't need to plan."

Stubbornly, Nicholas said, "I want to be sure that this is the best course of action for us."

There was a pause. Finally Lillian spoke. "Frankly, Nicholas," she said, "I'm insulted. We, I in particular, have been working very hard to support the museum."

Nicholas sighed. "Of course you have, Lillian. All I'm saying is, we haven't done any of the basic research to help us plan for another building."

"George Sloan laid it out for us in great detail."

"George laid out plans for the building, Lillian. I'm talking about plans for the historical society itself. What would we put *in* the building? Are there big stories that we should be telling that we aren't dealing with, and if so, what are they and what is the best way to tell them? We need to talk about priorities. There's a lot on the plate right now. If we decide to go forward, what do we drop? These are not simple issues. They need to be discussed in much greater depth, and we need to know all the consequences of our actions, in either direction, before we make any decisions."

"Are you saying that I, that we, don't understand the museum?"

Nicholas dabbed at his face. "All I'm saying is that, with your permission, I would like to do some more research on the building before we move any further. And I would like to schedule a retreat to discuss it, and even more important, what our plans should be for the future. I want the historical society to grow, but I want controlled growth, understood growth, strategically focused growth."

"Anything else?"

"Yes, I want a facilitator to help us through these issues."

"You want to hire someone so we can talk together?"

"Yes."

For Discussion

- What are the most important issues here?
- What are possible discussion topics for the retreat?
- If Lillian does not agree to a retreat, what should Nicholas do?
- What are the possible solutions to these issues?
- Why does Nicholas want to hire a consultant?
- What does the board need to focus on now, and why?

THE DINNER PARTY

Max Hanover always enjoyed going to the Hadleys' house for dinner. Fallon was an excellent cook, Jim had a superb cellar, and, almost as important, the people they gathered around their table were usually interesting. Tonight, there were three other couples besides he and Milly, and Max knew only one of them: Joe and Elise Collins, neighbors and fellow sailing enthusiasts. The others were Wade and Janet Baxter, antique collectors, and John and Margaret Otis, who ran the Holiday Travel Agency. Max never used a travel agency, and he had to be careful not to start talking about why. When he had an opinion—and he had one about travel agencies—he liked to share his views. He had embarrassed Milly more than once, but he was determined not to do it tonight.

"Dinner is served," said Fallon, coming into the room in a sweep of pale silk, her cheeks slightly flushed from working in the kitchen.

She's looking lovely, thought Max, and then guiltily looked over at Milly, chunkier but a lot nicer. Fallon had a bit of a competitive streak; that was why she had that little frown in her forehead. It was also why her dinners were always so good.

Max followed the others into the dining room. The table was set for 10, the crystal sparkled, the silver shined, and Fallon's Wedgwood plates added the final perfect touch. In the center of each plate was a large shallow bowl filled with a rich orange soup with a swirl of something white on top.

"Butternut squash soup," whispered Fallon as she walked by, "with crème fraiche."

Max nodded. He was a little overweight, but how bad could a little soup be?

As the guests pulled their chairs to the table. Jim leaned toward Max. "How's the museum, Max? Heard you're the new chairman of the board."

"The Science Museum?" Janet Baxter asked.

Max smiled, pleased that everyone now knew this piece of information; he was quite proud to have been elected. He had been surprised when the votes were counted and Marcus had fewer than he. Marcus had been angry, of course, and unfortunately had left the board, as had Alice Byrt, who seemed to admire him so much. "Yes," he said. "I take over the gavel next week."

"Why that's wonderful, Max," said Elise Collins, beaming at him. "You'll be able to make a real difference over there."

Max grinned, not sure what she meant but pleased by the compliment.

"Yes, they could use some help," said John Otis, glancing at Max and then looking at the others. "Margaret and I were over there last week and the place was so dreary. Nothing but pieces of scientific equipment—it all looks pretty much the same to me."

His wife nodded her head. "I remember that museum from when I was a girl. It sure hasn't changed much."

"Can't tamper with perfection," said Milly bravely, and Max's heart surged with love for her. He knew Milly was only standing up for him; she too thought the museum was a little on the dreary side.

"Is Carter Banning still there?" asked Wade Baxter. "Janet and I had some dealings with him a while back; he wanted to buy a collection of early measures we had acquired. Strange little man."

Max nodded. "Yes, Carter is still there. He's a good curator."

"He may be a good curator," said Janet, "but he's an odd one."

"Is he the one who plans those exhibits?" asked Joe Collins. "Elise and I took my parents to the museum when they visited us last month, and I'm afraid I'd have to agree with John, Max. The place was dreary. And that new exhibit, the one on telescopes, it read like a textbook."

Max began to feel uncomfortable. He didn't actually disagree with anything that had been said, it was just that he had never heard it before. The board, and the staff too, were so enthusiastic about the place. Board meetings were like testimonial dinners; Eugene Teagarten, the director always had a letter or two to share with the board, praising the museum or a staff member.

"Carter was the curator on that one," he said to Joe. "He's a well-recognized scholar you know, has a Ph.D., so maybe it was a little scholarly, but there's a lot of good information there. One of Carter's friends was visiting, he's a curator at some big museum in the North, and he was blown away by it."

"Maybe," said John, scraping the last of his soup out of the bowl, "but you couldn't prove it by me; I'd never read through all that stuff."

"Me either," said Margaret. "It was so boring."

"And you practically had to feel your way through the place." said John. "It's so dark in there."

Max shrugged, trying to resist the temptation to change the subject to travel agents. He said, "Maybe so, but the artifacts have to be protected; that's why we keep the light levels low. Some of those things are very valuable."

"I don't know, Max," said Fallon as she began to clear away the soup bowls. "Jim and I travel a lot, and we always go to the museums in other cities. They're not so dark and they seem to do things in a, well, in a more entertaining way," she said, almost apologetically. "Especially science museums—they're usually full of kids."

"How many visitors do you get over there?" asked Wade. "That's the way to tell whether the place is attracting people or not."

Max thought a moment and then said, "I don't remember." Actually, he did remember; the numbers were going down.

"Well, you should find out," said John. "I, for one, don't take people over there when they come to town any more; it just isn't worth the time."

This conversation was such a surprise to Max, he wasn't sure how to react. Sure, the museum was a little dusty, but isn't that how museums were supposed to be—quiet, old, and a little dark? He and Milly didn't go to museums all that much, probably because, now that he thought about it, they were quiet, old, and dark—a little spooky. But he knew it was good for the city to have a museum of such quality, and he was ready to support it with his time and even his money, if he had to. He wondered if any of the other board members had heard this kind of talk. Eugene hadn't mentioned anything, but maybe people were too polite to criticize the museum in front of its director. It seemed like no one at the table appreciated the museum. Not that he disagreed, exactly, but, well, the board had never talked about these things. And were they really important? This was hardly a representative group after all—just 10 people, eight if you excluded him and Milly. Still, it was odd dinner conversation; Max almost felt as if he had been attacked.

Fallon came in from the kitchen carrying a rib roast surrounded by roasted potatoes and carrots. She set it on the table and went back into the kitchen, returning with a large casserole of steamed asparagus and the best looking rolls that Max had ever seen.

"I made these myself," she said proudly, seeing Max eyeing the rolls.

"They look great," he said. "Remind me of the great rolls we get when we go to London. In fact, we're going next week, taking the whole family. Did Millie tell you, Fallon? You can get such great travel deals on the Internet; it's almost not worth it to stay home.

For Discussion

- Why doesn't Max, and presumably the director and board, already know how the community feels about the museum?
- There are just a few people attending this dinner party. Should Max pay attention to their comments?
- How will the museum and board know whether these criticisms are valid?
- What should the board do now?
- What should the museum do now?
- At what point should the board, the museum's CEO, and the museum's staff get together to discuss this issue?
- What should be the director's role?

Museum Definitions and Standards

In a most basic way, it is important for all museum trustees to understand the definition of a museum. Most definitions agree on the following characteristics —a museum must:

- be a legally organized not-for-profit institution or part of a not-for-profit institution or government entity;
- be essentially educational in nature;
- have a formally stated mission;
- have a staff member (paid or unpaid) who has museum knowledge and experience and is delegated authority and allocated sufficient financial resources to operate the museum effectively;
- present regularly scheduled programs and exhibits that use and interpret objects for the public according to accepted standards;
- have a formal and appropriate program of documentation, care, and use of collections and/or tangible objects;
- have a formal and appropriate program of presentation and maintenance of exhibits.

The museum field's most important designation of a high standard of museum performance is accreditation. To be accredited by the American Association of Museums, a museum must meet several operating criteria in addition to the definitional requirements outlined above. According to these criteria, the museum must:

- have been open to the public for at least two years;
- be open to the public at least 1,000 hours a year;
- have an operating budget of at least $25,000 per year.

The AAM accreditation process involves a rigorous process of organizational self-study and peer review designed to answer two core questions.

- How well does the museum achieve its stated mission and goals?
- How well does the museum's performance meet standards and practices as they are generally understood in the museum field?

In answering these questions AAM's Accreditation Commission looks carefully at issues of:

- Mission: An accreditable museum has a clear sense of mission and organizes all its activities in support of it.

- Governance: The governing authority is constituted, structured, and works by processes designed to advance the museum's mission.

- Collections Stewardship: The museum's collections are appropriate to the mission and are effectively managed in a way that supports their continued preservation and thoughtful utilization.

- Interpretation and Presentation: The museum's programs are designed and delivered in a way that advances the museum's mission and reaches the museum's audiences.

- Administration and Finances: The museum's financial and business practices are carried out in a way that advances its mission and are legal and ethical.

In making its determination as to whether a museum should be accredited, the Accreditation Commission depends on a variety of materials, including the museum's own self-study, descriptions of its staff, programs, and other activities, and an on-site peer visit to the museum that includes an interview with members of the board of trustees.

Of the approximately 16,000 museums in the United States, 750 were accredited as of November 2002.

Glossary of Museum Terms

The following definitions were compiled by AAM's Accreditation and Museum Assessment programs and reflect standard usage in the museum field.

ACCESSIONING: Formal process used to accept legally and record a specimen or artifact as a collection item. It involves the creation of an immediate, brief, and permanent record utilizing a control number or unique identifier for objects added to the collection from the same source at the same time, for which the institution accepts custody, right, or title.

AFFILIATE ORGANIZATION: Freestanding, separately incorporated organization (e.g., foundation or friends group).

AUDIENCE: Groups of people who use the museum's services. Audiences can be defined by the types of services they use and how they use them (e.g., visitors, subscribers, researchers, program participants, Web-site users), or by their demographic characteristics (e.g., families, school groups, seniors, culturally specific groups).

> **CURRENT AUDIENCE**: The groups or individuals who actually use the museum services.

> **POTENTIAL AUDIENCE**: Groups of people who could, but are not yet, using the museum's services.

> **TARGET AUDIENCE**: Groups of people the museum wants as primary users and for whom it designs programs and services.

AUDIENCE SURVEY/STUDY: Collecting data from the museum's actual and potential audiences to determine their composition. Used to assess the effectiveness of the museum's activities and services.

AUDIT: An examination of the records with the intent to verify, possibly including a reconciliation of objects to records or records to objects.

BYLAWS: Legal documents that describe matters delegated to the governing authority, such as membership categories, the logistics of scheduling and holding meetings of the corporation and the governing authority, committee charges, and provisions for amendments. Self-regulatory provisions for the governing authority, such as membership in the organization, attendance requirements, and termination, also are in the bylaws.

CATALOGUING: Creation of a full record of information about a specimen or artifact, cross-referenced to other records and files, including the process of identifying and documenting these objects in detail.

COLLABORATIVE EFFORT: A formal arrangement to work with other organizations on the planning, development, or implementation of exhibitions and public programming.

COLLECTING PLAN: A written document, approved by the governing authority, that details the scope of collecting by the museum and helps inform decisions regarding acquisition and deaccessioning.

COLLECTIONS: Groups of objects and their associated information, collected with purpose and maintained in order, managed in the public trust for the purpose of documentation, research, and education.

COLLECTIONS MANAGEMENT: All the activities that relate to the administration of a museum's collections. These include the deliberate planning, development, and documentation of collections.

COLLECTIONS MANAGEMENT POLICY: A written document, approved by the governing authority, that specifies the museum's policies concerning all collections-related issues, including accessioning, documentation, storage, and disposition.

COLLECTIONS PLAN: A plan guiding the content of the collections that leads the staff in a coordinated and uniform direction over a period of years to refine and expand the value of the collections

COMMUNITY: The geographic area (and its associated population) in which the museum exists.

DEACCESSIONING: Removing an accessioned object or group of objects from the museum's permanent collection through a formal process.

DIRECTORS AND OFFICERS LIABILITY INSURANCE: Insurance coverage for the exposure of directors, officers, and trustees to claims from donors, board members, beneficiaries, state attorneys general, staff, and others alleging mismanagement.

DOCENT: A person who teaches in a museum and is usually a volunteer.

EDUCATIONAL COLLECTIONS: Those that support the mission of the museum and are held and recorded separately from the permanent collection for use in exhibitions and public programs.

EXHIBITION: Group of exhibit components focused on an idea or theme. For a historic house or site, the restoration of an entire room or area would be equivalent; for a zoo or aquarium, the renovation of a collection area; for a botanical garden or arboretum, the redesign and replanting of a major area.

> **LONG-TERM EXHIBITION**: Generally thought of as permanent, remaining on view for longer than two years. Included in long-term exhibitions are presentations that change seasonally but use the same theme for more than two years.

> **TEMPORARY EXHIBITION**: On view for less than two years.

> **ORIGINATE**: Prepared partially or wholly under the supervision of the museum staff.

> **TRAVEL**: Sent to another museum or exhibition facility.

FIELD COLLECTING: For archaeological, biological, or paleontological material, the process of collecting material from its original site (e.g., archaeological or paleontological excavation).

FINANCIAL RESOURCES: The income and expenses of the museum.

FOCUS GROUP: Interview studies involving a carefully selected sample of eight to 10 individuals whose demographic and psychographic characteristics are of special interest to the museum. A planned but informal discussion carried out with the small group of visitors or community members to discuss a pre-determined topic in their own terms.

FORMATIVE EVALUATION: Testing carried out during development, including prototype building, testing comprehension of label copy, etc.

FRIEND/AUXILIARY: An organization whose purpose is to work solely on behalf of the museum.

FRONT-END EVALUATION: Collecting data from potential visitors to determine their level of interest and knowledge about a subject before an exhibition or program is developed.

FULL-TIME STAFF: Employees who work 35 hours or more per week.

GENERAL LIABILITY INSURANCE: Coverage that pertains, for the most part, to claims arising out of the insured's liability for injuries or damage caused by ownership of property, manufacturing operations, contracting operations, sale or distribution of products, and the operation of machinery, as well as professional services.

GOVERNING AUTHORITY: The executive body to which the director reports/is responsible. The entity that has legal and fiduciary responsibility for the museum (this body may not necessarily own the collection or the physical facility) and may include not-for-profit boards, appointed commissions, governmental bodies, and university regents. Names of governing authority include: Advisory Council, Board of Commissioners, Board of Directors, Board of Managers, Board of Regents, Board of Trustees, City Council, Commission.

HEAD OF GOVERNING AUTHORITY: The elected or appointed head of the executive body to which the director reports. *For institutions that are part of a larger non-museum parent organization, the head of the governing authority is considered to be the individual within the institution's larger parent organization to whom the director reports/is responsible (e.g., dean or provost of a university, director of parks and recreation for a city government, military post commander, etc.).*

HUMAN RESOURCES: All of the people, paid and unpaid, who regularly work at the museum.

INTERPRETATION: The media/activities through which a museum carries out its mission and educational role:

- Interpretation is a dynamic process of communication between the museum and the audience.
- Interpretation is the means by which the museum delivers its content.
- Interpretation media/activities include, but are not limited to: exhibits, tours, Web sites, classes, school programs, publications, outreach.

INVENTORY: An itemized listing of objects, often including current location, for which the museum has responsibility.

MEMBERS: Individuals, couples, families, corporations, and others enrolled in a program through which, in exchange for an annual dues payment, they receive museum benefits (such as free or reduced museum admission, invitations to exhibition openings or special events, a newsletter or other publications, and discounts at the museum shop).

MISSION: The mission statement defines the purpose of the museum and the means by which the museum achieves its purpose. The statement must be in accord with the purposes of the museum as enumerated in the basic legal documents.

MULTIPLE-SITE FACILITY: An organization with one or more non-contiguous sites in addition to a headquarters entity.

NONOPERATING REVENUES, SUPPORT, AND EXPENSES are applied to building or plant funds, purchases, the endowment or other nonoperating activities such as capital improvements, major renovation, long-term investment, fixed assets, and the purchase of objects for the collection.

OPERATING REVENUES, SUPPORT, AND EXPENSES are applied to the museum's general operations, such as exhibitions, education, conservation, collections management, research, training, development, and administration. Donor-restricted contributions that are specifically designated for ongoing museum operations should be included as operating funds.

PERMANENT COLLECTIONS: Those that are of intrinsic value to art, history, science, or culture and that support the mission of the museum and are held and curated by the museum.

PARENT ORGANIZATION: The overseeing organization (such as an historical society or university) that is responsible for the fiduciary control of the museum.

PART-TIME STAFF: Staff who work less than 35 hours per week.

PLANNING: The creation of policy and written plans. Thomas Wolf (*Managing a Nonprofit Organization*, 1990) lists two essential prerequisites of planning: 1) an evaluation/assessment of the organization's current position, and 2) a clear vision of the organization's future expressed through a statement of mission and goals. These prerequisites apply to all types of planning, whether it is long-range, disaster, exhibition, marketing, or program.

PUBLIC EXPERIENCE: What happens physically, intellectually, and emotionally to the public when it comes in contact with the museum either by word-of-mouth, through media references, or directly (visiting the museum).

PUBLIC INVOLVEMENT: When the public actively participates with and supports the museum financially and/or with physical presence, for example, as corporate sponsors, donors, trustees, advisors, visitors, volunteers, members, friends, or collaborators.

PUBLIC PERCEPTION: The public's impression, knowledge of, and feelings about the museum, which create an image for your museum and establish the role it has in the community.

PURPOSE: The museum's broad guiding principle as stated in its governing documents.

RESEARCH: Includes two types: applied—for the purpose of identification, reference, or solving a particular problem, or for acquiring information for the development of a program or publication; and pure—for the purpose of acquiring new knowledge or adding to knowledge. All museums are expected to engage in applied research; some museums may engage in pure research.

RESEARCH COLLECTIONS: Those held for comparative and study purposes.

REVENUE includes admission income, investment income and profit on the sale of investments or assets, membership fees, income from museum store/food service (gross), income from benefits and auxiliary activities, income from publications, tuition fees, performances, and all other sources not derived from contributions, grants, and parent organization support.

SPECIAL EVENTS: Concerts, festivals, or special seasonal programs.

SPECIAL EXHIBITIONS: Usually short-term, temporary exhibitions.

SUBSIDIARY ORGANIZATION: Controlled in its entirety by the parent museum for the purpose of providing service or support (includes auxiliaries).

SUMMATIVE EVALUATION: Determining the effectiveness of an exhibition or program after its installation.

SUPPORT includes federal grants, individual contributions, private foundation contributions and grants, cash corporate and business contributions and grants, state and local support (including federal funds administered by states), parent or sponsoring organization support, including cash payments made to the producers of goods or services provided to the museum without cost. Indirect cost allocations for maintenance, utilities, or services provided by the parent organization should also be included.

SUPPORTING GROUP: A group whose primary purpose is to support the museum, but who has no governance authority and responsibility for the museum. The group may provide financial support, volunteers, expertise, or advocacy to complement the knowledge and skills of the governing authority. Supporting groups may be called, for example, advisory boards, friends, guilds, or auxiliary boards.

> **INTERNAL SUPPORTING GROUPS** are part of the museum itself, either as an informal association or by appointment by the governing authority. They serve at the pleasure and under the direction of the museum's governing authority.

> **EXTERNAL SUPPORTING GROUPS** are informal associations or separately incorporated nonprofit entities. They are independent of the museum in their

own governance. Often there is a letter of understanding, a management agreement, or other document detailing the relationship between an external supporting group and the museum's governing authority.

TITLE: The possession of rights of ownership in personal property. Separate rights of possession include copyright interests, trademark rights, and any specific interest that the previous owner may have reserved.

TOURS: Any type of tour of the exhibitions; includes school, self, audio, and guided.

VISITOR EVALUATION: Obtaining valid and reliable information from visitors that helps in the planning of exhibitions and programs and in determining the extent to which the activities are meeting their intended objectives. Can include observation (tracking) studies, questionnaire, interviews, community meetings, and focus groups. Visitor evaluation can be carried out before (front end), during (formative), and after (summative) exhibition or program development.

VISITOR PROFILE SURVEY: Study or survey at the time a visitor enters or exits to determine demographic characteristics and nature of the visit and/or visitor behavior in the museum.

VISITOR SERVICES: Facilities or services that provide comfort to visitors, including the checkrooms, dining area, first aid stations, information, desk, restrooms, seating, signage, telephone booths, and water fountains.

VISITORS: Groups and individuals who go to the museum's physical facilities to use the museum services.

VOLUNTEER: An individual who offers time and service to the museum for no salary or wage.

WRITTEN AGREEMENT: Document between a museum and another organization (government agency, corporation, or another nonprofit organization) that defines ownership of assets (e.g., land, facilities, collections), fiscal responsibilities, employment and contractual arrangements, and lines of authority. A written agreement with a supporting group usually details the degree of autonomy for both parties in fiscal and programmatic matters. These documents are the bedrock of an organization's legal status.

Suggested Readings and Web-based Resources

The literature of nonprofit governance and management is immense. Rather than attempt an exhaustive bibliography, we offer instead a small selection of books here, some of which we have found personally useful in our work over the years. All of these titles provide practical guidance and/or solid context to the work of museum boards of trustees.

The Internet is an extraordinarily rich resource with very practical help for museum boards. With the simple typing of key words or concepts, board members will find essays, advice, guides, forms, templates, models, and matrices for almost any conceivable subject, problem, or need. We strongly urge those interested in deeper research into any of the topics mentioned in this book to avail themselves of this incredible resource.

Books and Articles

Adams, Roxana, ed. *Foundations of Museum Governance for Private, Nonprofit Museums.* American Association of Museums, 2002.

———. *Foundations of Governance for Museums in Non-Museum Parent Organizations.* American Association of Museums, 2002.

Fischer, Daryl, and Barbara Booker. *The Leadership Partnership.* Museum Trustee Association, 2002.

Magretta, Joan. *What Management Is: How It Works and Why It's Everyone's Business.* The Free Press, 2002.

Robinson, Maureen K. *Non-Profit Boards That Work: The End of One-Size-Fits-All Governance.* John Wiley & Sons, 2001.

———. *Developing the Nonprofit Board: Strategies for Orienting, Educating, and Motivating Board Members.* National Center for Nonprofit Boards, 1999.

Rutledge, Jennifer M. *Building Board Diversity*. National Center for Nonprofit Boards, 1994

Taylor, Barbara E., Richard P. Chait, and Thomas P. Holland. "The New Work of the Non-Profit Board," *Harvard Business Review*, September-October 1996, pp. 36-46.

General and Internet Resources

American Association of Museums. The association's Museum Assessment Program includes the Governance Assessment, which helps museum boards examine their structures, roles, and responsibilities and enhances their ability to advance the institution's mission and engage in effective planning. www.aam-us.org

Association of Governing Boards of Universities and Colleges. While focused on the boards of colleges and universities, the AGB has a variety of resources of interest to all non-profit boards. www.agb.org

BoardSource (formally the National Center for Nonprofit Boards) publishes a variety of materials of interest to museum boards. www.boardsource.org

Charities Review Council of Minnesota. This site has a good discussion of conflict of interest policies as well as other useful links. www.crcmn.org

Museum Trustee Association publishes a variety of materials that can be very helpful to museum boards. www.mta-hq.org

The Authors

HAROLD AND SUSAN SKRAMSTAD bring a broad and deep perspective to the subject of museum trusteeship. Harold has been active in the museum field for more than 30 years. He has held senior management positions at the Smithsonian Institution's National Museum of American History, and served as director of the Chicago Historical Society, president of Henry Ford Museum & Greenfield Village, and as a trustee of a variety of museums and other nonprofit organizations. Susan has worked primarily in the area of higher education, serving as executive assistant to the chancellor and vice chancellor for institutional advancement at the University of Michigan's Dearborn campus. Susan presently serves as the chairman of the board of trustees of the New Mexico Endowment for the Humanities. Harold presently serves as a director of the New Mexico State University Foundation and as a trustee of the New Mexico Museum of Natural History and Science. For the last seven years, the Skramstads have served as consultants to numerous nonprofit organizations on issues of strategic and interpretive planning, board development, team building, and fund raising.

Index

V

W